APPLES *of* GOLD
IN
PICTURES *of* SILVER

PROMISES FROM GOD

BILLIE KAYE TSIKA

DESTINY IMAGE® PUBLISHERS, INC.

PO Box 310, Shippensburg, PA 17257-0310

"Promoting Inspired Lives."

This book and all other Destiny Image and Destiny Image Fiction books are available at Christian bookstores and distributors worldwide.

For more information on foreign distributors, call 717-532-3040.

Reach us on the Internet: www.destinyimage.com.

ISBN 13 TP: 978-0-7684-6384-2
ISBN 13 eBook: 978-0-7684-6385-9

For Worldwide Distribution, Printed in the USA
1 2 3 4 5 6 7 8 / 26 25 24 23 22

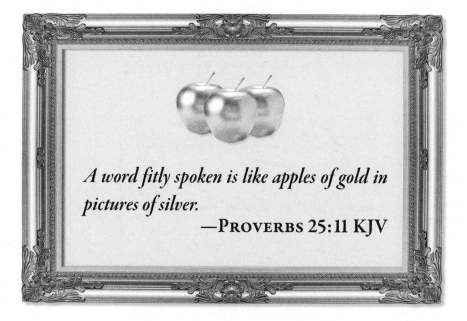

A word fitly spoken is like apples of gold in pictures of silver.

—Proverbs 25:11 KJV

God's Promises

What God has promised He will do.
Because those promises are meant for you.
His word alone is His to give,
He gives that word so you might live.
For every challenge faced today
God has a promise you can pray.
But prayer alone is not the end,
By faith that promise will then begin.
You'll see that promise as it unfolds
And know for certain that you've been told,
That Christ Himself has made them real
And from your heart no one can steal.
So get your word from God today
And stand on it and never stray.
Cause what He said, He will perform
And for His child it will be the norm.

—Paul Tsika, 2021

CONTENTS

INTRODUCTION

Cross my heart and hope to die! I don't remember how many times I promised this as a child when someone asked me to keep a secret and said, "Promise you won't tell anyone? Cross your heart and hope to die if you do." Do you remember saying this? I certainly do! Of course, I would have one hand behind my back with my fingers crossed, which I thought made the promise null and void. In other words, I didn't intend to keep my promise because it was much too "juicy" to keep it to myself. I wanted people to think I knew something they didn't. If and when I did tell their secret, I would say, "Now, this is very confidential! Don't tell anyone!" RIGHT! I didn't have a problem keeping a secret or my promises, but those I told certainly did!

Well, there is One who is faithful to keep every promise (covenants) He makes. We can read of His faithfulness all through the Bible. From the Old Testament to the New, God keeps His promises.

*Therefore know [without any doubt] and under-
stand that the LORD your God, He is God, the
faithful God, who is keeping His covenant and His
[steadfast] lovingkindness to a thousand generations
with those who love Him and keep His commandments* (Deuteronomy 7:9 AMP).

Paul David Tripp says, "If you are going to reach for the life-giving promises of the gospel, you must also celebrate the absolute rule of the One who, because of His rule, is able to deliver those promises to you. Hope is not found just in the beauty of those promises, but in the incalculable power and authority of the One who has made them. There is no hope in the promises of one who has little hope because your Lord has complete rule over all the places where you will need His promises to become reality."[1]

Tripp points out that God not only makes promises that sustain our hope, but He has the character to keep them. Not only does God make promises, He has the wherewithal—the power, authority, and desire—to see them through. Our God does not make His promises lightly with one hand behind His back and His fingers crossed, and knowing God's word is good makes us hunger to experience the promises He speaks.

When our children were very young, I would put scripture to music. This made it so easy to memorize. I wanted them to remember the promises of God. One of the verses I taught them was Numbers 23:19 (KJV):

*God is not a man, that he should lie; neither the son
of man, that he should repent: hath he said, and*

shall he not do it? or hath he spoken, and shall he not make it good?

I don't know if they remember this verse after all these years, but I sure do! God cannot lie! Once He has spoken something, He will do it. Hallelujah for God's promises to us who love Him, and to those He loves.

In this book I share some promises God has spoken to my heart through the years. I have stood on these during some very rough times, and even during the best of times. His promises are available in every situation of life; beautiful and exciting or challenging and devastating, God was with me through them all!

Are you struggling with something that seems to keep you living in fear? God has promised peace to His children. Doubt? He has a promise for you. Depression? He will give hope. Worry? He gives peace that passes all understanding. Anger? God will calm your heart. Unforgiveness? His forgiveness is available. Bitterness? Jealousy? Envy? Grief? God has a promise for everything you are struggling with in this life. God's "living" Word will come "alive" to you as you trust Him. He will speak to you! After all, His Holy Spirit lives in you. I call God's Word His Love Letters to me, but His love letters are to you also, to every child of God.

As Charles Spurgeon writes,

> You take a divine promise, spoken thousands of years ago, and lo, it is fulfilled to you! It becomes as true to you as if God had spoken it for the first time this very day, and you were the person to whom it was addressed.[2]

Apples of Gold in Pictures of Silver will open God's promises to you and help them become part of your daily life. His promises are sweet to taste, and like precious gold and silver, they only increase in value. His word is the truth you can rest upon. It will illuminate the journey He has put before you.

> *Your word is a lamp to my feet and a light for my path* (Psalm 119:105).

ENDNOTES

1. Paul David Tripp, *New Morning Mercies: A Daily Gospel Devotional* (Wheaton, IL: Crossway, 2014).

2. Charles Spurgeon Quotes, @https://theblazingcenter.com/2018/10/charles-spurgeon-quotes.html; accessed November 8, 2021.

Chapter 1

ETERNAL LIFE: THE MOST IMPORTANT PROMISE OF ALL

For God so loved the world that he gave his one and only Son, that whoever believes in him shall not perish but have eternal life.

—JOHN 3:16 NIV

Perhaps the most important promise that our Lord gives us is eternal life. Think about it. It is the promise of eternal life that leads us into the arms of our Lord right from the beginning. Where is the hope, rest, and joy of this life without the promise of eternal life? What would all the other promises stand upon if our life ever after with Christ, His purpose on earth with all of its agony, was shattered? But this promise is not flimsy and breakable; it is steadfast. We can run to Him assured that His arms are open and Heaven awaits us. And, when we open our arms to Jesus and become immersed in His heart, only then does our deeper purpose on earth begin to reveal itself. Paul David Tripp talks about the safety and faithfulness behind His call to us.

> God is amazing in His wisdom, abundant in His grace, and boundless in His love. He is saving, forgiving, transforming, and delivering. What He says is always best and what He requires is always good. What He calls you to do, He empowers by His grace. When He guides, He protects. He stands with power and faithfulness behind every one of His promises. He has never failed to deliver anything that He has promised. There is simply no risk in answering the call of the King of Kings.[1]

This promise of eternal life is probably the first verse most children in church memorize; *whoever believes in Him (Christ) should not perish but have everlasting life.* I memorized this promise when I was six years old. My mom and dad had been saved, so we started going to church. Vacation Bible School was a "must attend" when I was young. I learned many songs and, of course, this precious promise of everlasting life. I wasn't a Christian at this time, but in due season, God worked a miracle in my heart and saved me by His grace.

In Acts 16, Paul and Silas are beaten and put in jail for preaching in Jesus' name. Around midnight, as they sang praises to God, an earthquake opened the prison doors and set all the prisoners loose from their chains. The jailer was going to kill himself because he thought all the prisoners had escaped. Paul called out to him to let him know no one had escaped.

The jailer fell to his knees and asked, "What must I do to be saved?" They said, *"Believe on the Lord Jesus Christ and you will be saved, not only you, but your household, also."* Paul and Silas then shared God's Word with the jailer and his family and they all believed and were baptized. Notice their part was to believe. Grace was already provided.

The gospel (good news) has enough power in itself to convert the lost. You are saved by grace alone, through faith alone, in Christ alone. No amount of good works can save a person. No amount of self-sacrifice can merit us Heaven. No amount of giving can take us closer to Heaven. We can try, try, try to work our way to Heaven, but the only way is through the cross of Jesus. He, our ultimate sacrifice, is the way, the truth and the life. No man, woman, boy or girl can get to the Father but by Him (John 14:6).

Many times we speak as though we are responsible for our salvation. Little do we realize that all circumstances and events are orchestrated by God Himself to bring us *to* Himself. The following excerpt points out how God is in *pursuit of us.*

> Many personal salvation testimonies go something like this: "I heard the gospel of Jesus Christ; I decided to open my life to Him; I came to Jesus; I gave him my heart; I received Him; I repented of my sins; I decided to follow Jesus." Note the continual use of the perpendicular pronoun "I" as if it all depended upon me. When we get to heaven, we will find out how little we had to do with our salvation and how true this verse today is "He who

began a good work in you." Salvation is, from start to finish, from first to last, the work of God Himself in us. He sought us. He found us. He began the good work in us. He keeps us. And one day He will present us faultless before His Father's throne. The origin of our salvation lies not within us but with God Himself. He takes the initiative. He convicts us of sin. He convinces us of our righteousness in Him. He calls us out of darkness into His marvelous light. He redeems us for His own. Yes, He began the good work in us.

—AUTHOR UNKNOWN

My part is simply to believe on the Lord Jesus Christ and I shall be saved.

You may think you're past saving; you've made too many wrong choices; you've sinned too much for God to rescue you, or that you have nothing to give in return for the gift of salvation the Lord offers you. Charlotte Elliott, even as the daughter of a minister, heard of grace, spoke about grace, but did not grasp its reality in the conversion experience. Charlotte's physical condition was frail and weak and she was frustrated. She could think of nothing she had or could do that would make her worthy of the promise of eternal life that Jesus held out to her. Little did Charlotte know that a deeper purpose for her would reveal itself after she came to Him with empty hands. Her conversion experience itself would provide a response that would touch the world for generations to come. Charlotte's story follows.

Charlotte Elliott was not sure of her relationship with Christ. She wasn't sure how to be saved, yet she was the daughter of a minister. She heard an evangelist ask, "Are you at peace with God?" When she saw the evangelist a few weeks later she told him she couldn't get his question off her mind. What could she possibly bring to God? He simply replied that she didn't need to bring anything but herself. She gladly accepted Christ.

Years later, in 1835, crippled by illness and constant fatigue, she was unable to help a local church's cause. But there was something she could do. She sat down and wrote this poem to encourage others who may have nothing to bring.

Just as I am, without one plea
But that Thy blood was shed for me
And that Thou bidst me come to Thee
Oh, Lamb of God, I come, I come.

Her poem was published, and she was bombarded with requests for it. She was thrilled to know that the poem was being sold and the money was going to the church she wanted to help. Her poem became a song that has been translated into hundreds of languages and published in more than 1,600 hymnals. Sixty years later, in 1931, a 31-year-old man riding in the sidecar of his brother's motorcar came to the end of his internal struggle against whether Christ was indeed the Son of God. He finally knew in his soul that indeed Jesus was just who He said He was. He realized that God calls us to Him "just as we are." When C.S. Lewis stepped out of the sidecar, he was a new man, saved by grace.

Nearly ninety-nine years after Charlotte penned her words, and 3 years after Lewis' conversion, the 16-year-old son of a dairy farmer listened intently as he heard the message of salvation preached at a revival service in Charlotte, NC. When the song, "Just As I Am" was sung at the end, young Billy Graham went forward to accept Christ.

Twenty years later, Billy Graham had become a successful evangelist and was invited to speak at Cambridge University in England. He was so nervous that he almost canceled it. But he was introduced to a kind man named C.S. Lewis who encouraged him to disregard the critics who had spoken against him. Rev. Graham went on to speak to an overflow crowd of 2,000 each night of the revival, and when he returned to England in 1989, he addressed a crowd of 80,000 at England's Wembley Stadium. As always, he closed the event with the same song that brought him to Christ, "Just as I Am."

When you think you have nothing to bring to Jesus, you are right! Nothing but yourself. He wants you, just as you are! He can take frustration like Charlotte's, skepticism like Lewis', and nervousness like Billy Graham to reach the world through you.

"Just as I am, though tossed about
With many a conflict, many a doubt
Fightings within and fears without
O Lamb of God, I Come, I Come!"[2]

Let me encourage you, as one saved by grace, to seek those things that are above, where Christ is seated at the right hand of God. Let's set our minds on things that are ours for eternity, not things of this world that will soon pass away. After all, we are eternal beings. We are going to live somewhere for all eternity. Where will you spend eternity? Cast your care on the Lord and come just as you are and let Him change you.

My precious mother went to Heaven in 2000. After her funeral, I went to North Carolina to stay with Thom and Kelley, our son and his wife. Our granddaughter, Shelby, was four years old at this time. When we went to lunch after church, Shelby began asking me questions about where my mother was and so many questions about Heaven. I elaborated on what Heaven was like and how wonderful it was that my mother was with Jesus. On the way home from the restaurant, I looked to the back of the car where Shelby was sitting in her car seat. She had her head bowed, so I asked what she was doing. She looked up and with great gusto and passion said, "I'm telling Jesus, I believe in Him, I believe in Him." How else can we respond when someone asks us about our faith?

You, alone, are the Savior of the world. Take my life and use me for Your glory. You, my LORD, are "my rock, and my fortress, and my deliverer; my God, my strength, in whom I will trust; my buckler, and the horn of my salvation, and my high tower. I will call upon [You, LORD], because you are worthy to be praised..." (Psalm 18:2-3 KJV). Amen.

PROMISES TO MEMORIZE OR MEDITATE UPON

These things have I written unto you that believe on the name of the Son of God; that ye may know that ye have eternal life, and that ye may believe on the name of the Son of God (1 John 5:13 KJV).

That if you confess with your mouth the Lord Jesus and believe in your heart that God has raised Him from the dead, you will be saved. For with the heart one believes unto righteousness, and with the mouth confession is made unto salvation (Romans 10:9-10 NKJV).

Most assuredly, I say to you, he who hears My word and believes in Him who sent Me has everlasting life, and shall not come into judgment, but has passed from death into life (John 5:24).

Then he called for a light, and sprang in, and came trembling, and fell down before Paul and Silas, and brought them out, and said, Sirs, what must I do to be saved? And they said, Believe on the Lord Jesus Christ, and thou shalt be saved, and thy house (Acts 16:29-31 KJV).

For by grace are ye saved through faith; and that not of yourselves: it is the gift of God: Not of works, lest any man should boast (Ephesians 2:8-9 KJV).

And Jesus looking upon them saith, With men it is impossible, but not with God: for with God all things are possible (Mark 10:37 KJV).

But when the goodness and loving kindness of God our Savior appeared, he saved us, not because of works done by us in righteousness, but according to his own mercy, by the washing of regeneration and renewal of the Holy Spirit, whom he poured out on us richly through Jesus Christ our Savior, so that being justified by his grace we might become heirs according to the hope of eternal life (Titus 3:4-7 ESV).

For if while we were enemies we were reconciled with God through the death of His Son, much more, having been reconciled, we shall be saved by His life (Romans 5:10 NASB).

Prayer

Lord, I surrender my life to You, my Blessed Redeemer. You, alone, have the keys to eternal life. You, alone, are the Savior of the world. Take my life and use me for Your glory. "The LORD is my rock, and my fortress, and my deliverer; my God, my strength, in whom I will trust; my buckler, and the horn of my salvation, and my high tower. I will call

upon the LORD, who is worthy to be praised..."
(Psalm 18:2-3 KJV). Amen.

What promise has God given you today?

JUNGYUN LEE

In him we have obtained an inheritance, having been predestined according to the purpose of him who works all things according to the counsel of his will (Ephesians 1:11 ESV).

If I had the gift of prophecy, and if I understood all of God's secret plans and possessed all knowledge, and if I had such faith that I could move mountains, but didn't love others, I would be nothing (1 Corinthians 13:2 NLT).

This year, I will be turning fifty years of age and have reached the halfway mark of my life (who knows?). Throughout my first half, I pursued personal success and sought out wisdom and knowledge through my experiences. However, during my second half, I want to pursue not just an understanding of Jesus' love, but I also want to feel it in my heart. I want to implement His love in my knowledge and wisdom to make a more meaningful impact on the people that I touch.

ASHLEA TOMS

I can do all things through Christ who strengthens me (Philippians 4:13 NKJV).

I hold onto this promise because it encourages me that no matter what is happening in life, He is there with me and will strengthen and guide me through it.

BONNIE MARSHALL

And let us not be weary in well doing: for in due season we shall reap, if we faint not (Galatians 6:9).

What this has meant to me is that we are going to be disappointed, discouraged, tired, frustrated, etc., "weary," if you will, in doing good because doing good is not easy. But it is worth it, and we will be blessed and reap a reward even bigger than we can imagine if we will continue to make right choices. Losing yourself in the service of others with love is the key. I've seen this example in others and I try to emulate that myself.

ENDNOTES

1. Paul David Tripp, *New Morning Mercies: A Daily Gospel Devotional,* (Wheaton, IL: Crossway, 2014).

2. The Story of Just As I Am, Contributed by Dr. Larry Petton, December 17, 2019. https://www .sermoncentral.com/sermon-illustrations/100553/ the-story-of-just-as-i-am-by-dr-larry-petton; accessed November 8, 2021.

Chapter 2

SANCTIFIED: HE IS FAITHFUL!

And I am sure of this, that he who began a good work in you will bring it to completion at the day of Jesus Christ.

—PHILIPPIANS 1:6 ESV

This promise gives us such hope; God WILL be faithful and continue to transform (sanctify) us until we are with Him in glory. The apostle Paul was talking to the Christians at Philippi when he said, "I am persuaded of this. I am certain of this." Paul had no doubt that the God who launched a good work in the Philippians, would continue it. God never starts anything that He cannot finish. He will see it through to completion. In Romans 9, we read that God is the Potter, we are the clay. God is the one who shapes us, molds us, and makes us into His image. He is the One who began the work in us, and as I said before, He is the One who will complete this work in us.

This transformation/sanctification is a lifetime process. Just as we grow in our human bodies, we grow in our spiritual walk with Christ. Sometimes we expect baby Christians to mature much faster than they do...as if we do! A one-year-old can't be 20 years old no matter what we think or say. We all must go through our normal growth pattern in our bodies, ages and spiritual walk. So, let's not expect baby Christians to mature so quickly. Patience and grace should be given to all, just as it's given to us. The late C. S. Lewis once remembered,

> When I was a child, I often had a toothache, and I knew that if I went to my mother, she would give me something which would deaden the pain for that night and let me get to sleep. But I did not go to my mother—at least not till the pain became very bad. And the reason I did not go was this: I did not doubt she would give me the aspirin; but I knew she would also do something else. I knew she would take me to the dentist the next morning. I could not get what I wanted out of her without getting something more, which I did not want. I wanted immediate relief from my pain; but I could not get it without having my teeth set permanently right. And I knew those dentists; I knew they would start fiddling about with all sorts of other teeth which had not yet begun to ache. Our Lord is like the dentists. Dozens of people go to him to

be cured of some particular sin. Well, he will cure it all right, but he will not stop there. That may be all you asked; but if you once call him in, he will give you the full treatment.[1]

As I look back on my journey in this Christian life, I marvel at God's patience and grace toward me. I think of all the words I spouted as though I knew so much when it came to matters of the Lord. In this last season of my life I know God has to laugh at my ignorance. However, He has been patient, kind, long-suffering, and gracious to me. I told Paul back in the 1980s, when we were struggling in so many areas, that I believe God lets us talk and pontificate for a few years after we are saved, then one day He says, "Alright, now I'm going to let you see how much you really believe!" He allows struggles and trials to enter our lives to bring us to a reality of what we truly believe as a born-again believer, and to give us a heart of compassion and love. I'm not saying this is fact, but this is how I saw it when I was brought to my knees. He continually works His grace in our hearts daily. Like I said, He is patient! He's not in a hurry. His timing is not our timing. He's an On-Time God!

A.W. Tozer, an American pastor, author, and spiritual mentor, said, "There are rare Christians whose very presence incites others to be better Christians. I want to be that rare Christian."[2] I want God to so sanctify me that I too will be that Christian. There's an old hymn written by B.B. McKinney that says, "While passing through this world of sin, and others your life shall view, Be clean and pure without, within, Let others see Jesus in you."[3] Our life is a book that people read. Are we pointing them to Jesus? We should so live that the light of our lives points them to the cross of Christ.

In his book *Daily Meditations*, Tripp compares our journey of sanctification to entering into the vision of a heavenly father:

> It is only when you understand the completeness of your justification (that your penalty has been paid and you have been made eternally right with God by the life and death of Jesus) that you are able to rest in the ongoing discipline of your sanctification. That discipline is not to make you right with God, but an expression of the fact that you have been made right with God, and because you have, you are now the object of his fatherly love. You can expect his discipline, but you do not have to fear his anger. You will experience his correction, but you will never face his rejection. He disciplines all his children in order to produce a harvest of righteousness, but he will never punish you for your sin. *"For indeed Christ died for sins once for all, the Just and Righteous for the unjust and unrighteous [the Innocent for the guilty] so that He might bring us to God, having been put to death in the flesh, but made alive in the Spirit"* (1 Peter 3:18). Amen and Amen[4]

Tripp makes the point that the discipline of a father is not so that one can enter his family, but because he or she is already in the family. A good, good father "grows up" a child so that he is complete and lacking nothing for life and godliness (see 2 Peter 1:3).

Paul prays and assures us that God is faithful to our completion.

> *Now may the God of Peace make you holy* [sanctify you] *in every way, and may your whole spirit and soul and body be kept blameless until the Lord Jesus Christ comes again. God will make this happen, for he who calls you is faithful* (1 Thessalonians 5:23-25 NLT).

PROMISES TO MEMORIZE OR MEDITATE UPON

> *The Lord will perfect that which concerns me* (Psalm 138:8 NKJV).
> *And we know that all things work together for good to those who love God, to those who are the called according to His purpose. For whom He foreknew, He also predestined to be conformed to the image of His Son, that He might be the firstborn among many brethren...* (Romans 8:29 NKJV).
> *He chose us in Him before the foundation of the world, that we should be holy and without blame before Him in love* (Ephesians 1:4 NKJV).

Prayer

> Father, thank You for Your promise to work in my life to make me more like Jesus. Thank You for continually using everything in my life to teach me Your ways. I praise You for Your faithfulness. I yield myself to You and Your complete work in me.

"Lord, sanctify me through your truth, your word is truth" (see John 17:17). Amen.

What promise has God given to you today?

LAURIE DUNCAN

God is our refuge and strength, a helper who is always found in times of trouble (Psalm 46:1 NKJV).

A refuge is a safe place, a trusted place or person. It is something or someone you can run to that will take care of you and make you feel safe and secure. When we choose to take refuge in God, we are giving that trust to Him—choosing to believe He is our safe place, our strength and helper. We trust His promises and His ways.

VANESSA CRANDELL

God is within her, she will not fall; God will help her at break of day (Psalm 46:5 NIV).

What a wonderful opportunity to let go and let God. Being a wife, mother, sister and friend to so many cherished people in my life, I have realized and accepted that the more I know, the more I realize I don't know, and the more I realize I am not in control. This immeasurable uncertainty opens a true connection to me and my Savior Jesus Christ and this Bible promise provides the ultimate confirmation. It gives and brings great joy and an unexplainable peace of mind just to glance at this promise.

ENDNOTES

1. C.S. Lewis, *Mere Christianity,* (New York, NY: Touchstone, 1996), 173-174.

2. Top quotes by Aiden Wilson Tozer, https://www.quotemaster.org/author/Aiden+Wilson+Tozer; accessed November 8, 2021.

3. Hymn—"Let Others See Jesus in You," https:/hymnary.org/text/while_passing_through_this_world_of_sin; accessed November 8, 2021.

4. Paul David Tripp, *New Morning Mercies: A Daily Gospel Devotional* (Wheaton, IL: Crossway, 2014).

Chapter 3

FORGIVENESS: GOD IS MERCY

If we confess our sins, He is faithful and just to forgive
us our sins, and to cleanse us from all unrighteous-
ness. If we say that we have not sinned, we make
Him a liar, and His word is not in us.

—1 John 1:9-10 NKJV

Who is merciful to forgive our sins? God is merciful. Mercy is the love of God expressed for the need of man. Mercy flows from God's goodness (see Exodus 34: 5-6). Jesus is God's mercy to mankind as the atoning sacrifice for our sins. He was given to endure our suffering as the exchange for forgiveness for all mankind—if we choose to accept it. When we do, we are cleansed and changed so that we no longer think and act like the world. Man's natural inclination is not to forgive but to condemn or demand justice. We even condemn ourselves. Self will never let us off the hook, but will continually remind us of our sin. We must accept *His* forgiveness instead of trying to convince ourselves that we need to forgive ourselves. The psalmist says, *"As far as the east is from the west, so far has He removed our transgressions from us"* (Psalm 103:12 NKJV).

Paul tells us plainly that there is *"now no condemnation for those who are in Christ Jesus"* (Romans 8:1 NKJV). He also says that *"if anyone is in Christ, he is a new creation; old things have passed away; behold, all things have become new"* (2 Corinthians 5:17). Unlike man's inclination toward justice and condemnation, God's nature is mercy. Once we know and truly experience the depth of God's mercy, we will be moved to forgive.

> Free, full, sovereign pardon is in the hand of the great King: it is his prerogative to forgive, and he delights to exercise it. Because his nature is mercy, and because he has provided a sacrifice for sin, therefore forgiveness is with him for all that come to him confessing their sins. The power of pardon is permanently resident with God: he has forgiveness ready in his hand at this instant. "That thou mayest be feared." This is the fruitful root of piety. None fear the Lord like those who have experienced his forgiving love. Gratitude for pardon produces far more fear and reverence of God than all the dread which is inspired by punishment.[1]

Corrie ten Boom was a Dutch Christian who, along with her family, helped nearly 800 Jews escape the Nazi Holocast during World War II. After being betrayed and imprisoned by German authorities, the entire family was shipped to concentration camps where only Corrie survived under the harsh conditions and atrocities. In her book *The Hiding Place,* Corrie relates her struggle and then her freedom to forgive her captors.

> It was in a church in Munich that I saw him, a balding heavyset man in a gray overcoat, a brown felt hat clutched between his hands. People were filing out of the basement room where I had just spoken, moving along the rows of wooden chairs to the door at the rear.
>
> It was 1947 and I had come from Holland to defeated Germany with the message that God forgives.
>
> It was the truth they needed most to hear in that bitter, bombed-out land, and I gave them my favorite mental picture. Maybe because the sea is never far from a Hollander's mind, I liked to think that that's where forgiven sins were thrown.
>
> "When we confess our sins," I said, "God casts them into the deepest ocean, gone forever."
>
> The solemn faces stared back at me, not quite daring to believe. There were never questions after a talk in Germany in 1947. People stood up in silence, in silence collected their wraps, in silence left the room.
>
> And that's when I saw him, working his way forward against the others. One moment I saw the overcoat

and the brown hat: the next, a blue uniform and a visored cap with its skull and crossbones.

It came back with a rush: the huge room with its harsh overhead lights, the pathetic pile of dresses and shoes in the center of the floor, the shame of walking naked past this man. I could see my sister's frail form ahead of me, ribs sharp beneath the parchment skin. Betsie, how thin you were!

Betsie and I had been arrested for concealing Jews in our home during the Nazi occupation of Holland; this man had been a guard at Ravensbrück concentration camp where we were sent.

Now he was in front of me, hand thrust out: "A fine message, fräulein! How good it is to know that, as you say, all our sins are at the bottom of the sea!"

And I, who had spoken so glibly of forgiveness, fumbled in my pocketbook rather than take that hand. He would not remember me, of course—how could he remember one prisoner among those thousands of women?

But I remembered him and the leather crop swinging from his belt. It was the first time since my release that I had been face to face with one of my captors and my blood seemed to freeze.

"You mentioned Ravensbrück in your talk," he was saying. "I was a guard in there." No, he did not remember me.

"But since that time," he went on, "I have become a Christian. I know that God has forgiven me for the cruel things I did there, but I would like to hear it from your lips as well. Fräulein"—again the hand came out—"will you forgive me?"

And I stood there—I whose sins had every day to be forgiven—and could not. Betsie had died in that place—could he erase her slow terrible death simply for the asking?

It could not have been many seconds that he stood there, hand held out, but to me it seemed hours as I wrestled with the most difficult thing I had ever had to do.

For I had to do it—I knew that. The message that God forgives has a prior condition: that we forgive those who have injured us. "If you do not forgive men their trespasses," Jesus says, "neither will your Father in heaven forgive your trespasses."

I knew it not only as a commandment of God, but as a daily experience. Since the end of the war, I had had a home in Holland for victims of Nazi brutality. Those who were able to forgive their former enemies were able also to return to the outside world and rebuild their lives, no matter what the physical scars. Those who nursed their bitterness remained invalids. It was as simple and as horrible as that.

And still I stood there with the coldness clutching my heart. But forgiveness is not an emotion—I knew that too. Forgiveness is an act of the will, and the will can function regardless of the temperature of the heart.

"Jesus, help me!" I prayed silently. "I can lift my hand. I can do that much. You supply the feeling."

And so woodenly, mechanically, I thrust my hand into the one stretched out to me. And as I did, an incredible thing took place. The current started in my shoulder, raced down my arm, sprang into our joined hands. And then this healing warmth seemed to flood my whole being, bringing tears to my eyes.

"I forgive you, brother!" I cried. "With all my heart!"

For a long moment we grasped each other's hands, the former guard and the former prisoner. I had never known God's love so intensely as I did then.

And having thus learned to forgive in this hardest of situations, I never again had difficulty in forgiving: I wish I could say it! I wish I could say that merciful and charitable thoughts just naturally flowed from me from then on. But they didn't.

If there's one thing I've learned at 80 years of age, it's that I can't store up good feelings and behavior—but only draw them fresh from God each day.

Maybe I'm glad it's that way. For every time I go to Him, He teaches me something else. I recall the time, some 15 years ago, when some Christian friends whom I loved and trusted did something which hurt me.

You would have thought that having forgiven the Nazi guard; this would have been child's play. It wasn't. For weeks I seethed inside. But at last, I asked God again to work His miracle in me. And again, it happened: first the cold-blooded decision, then the flood of joy and peace.

I had forgiven my friends; I was restored to my Father.

Then, why was I suddenly awake in the middle of the night, hashing over the whole affair again? My friends! I thought. People I loved! If it had been strangers, I wouldn't have minded so.

I sat up and switched on the light. "Father, I thought it was all forgiven! Please help me do it!"

But the next night I woke up again. They'd talked so sweetly too! Never a hint of what they were planning. "Father!" I cried in alarm. "Help me!"

His help came in the form of a kindly Lutheran pastor to whom I confessed my failure after two sleepless weeks.

"Up in that church tower," he said, nodding out the window, "is a bell which is rung by pulling on a rope. But you know what? After the sexton lets go of the rope, the bell keeps on swinging. First ding then dong. Slower and slower until there's a final dong and it stops.

"I believe the same thing is true of forgiveness. When we forgive someone, we take our hand off the rope. But if we've been tugging at our grievances for a long time, we mustn't be surprised if the old angry thoughts keep coming for a while. They're just the ding-dongs of the old bell slowing down."

And so, it proved to be. There were a few more midnight reverberations, a couple of dings when the subject came up in my conversation. But the force—which was my willingness in the matter—had gone out of them. They came less and less often and at last stopped altogether.

And so, I discovered another secret of forgiveness: that we can trust God not only above our emotions, but also above our thoughts.

And still, He had more to teach me, even in this single episode. Because many years later, in 1970, an American with whom I had shared the ding-dong principle came to visit me in Holland and met the people involved. "Aren't those the friends who let you down?" he asked as they left my apartment.

"Yes," I said a little smugly. "You can see it's all forgiven."

"By you, yes," he said. "But what about them? Have they accepted your forgiveness?"

"They say there's nothing to forgive! They deny it ever happened. But I can prove it!" I went eagerly to my desk. "I have it in black and white! I saved all their letters, and I can show you where—"

"Corrie!" My friend slipped his arm through mine and gently closed the drawer. "Aren't you the one whose sins are at the bottom of the sea? And are the sins of your friends etched in black and white?" For an anguishing moment, I could not find my voice. "Lord Jesus," I whispered at last, "who takes all my sins away, forgive me for preserving all these years the evidence against others! Give me grace to burn all the blacks and whites as a sweet-smelling sacrifice to Your glory."

I did not go to sleep that night until I had gone through my desk and pulled out those letters— curling now with age—and fed them all into my little coal-burning grate. As the flames leaped and glowed, so did my heart.

"Forgive us our trespasses," Jesus taught us to pray, "as we forgive those who trespass against us." In the ashes of those letters, I was seeing yet another facet of His mercy. What more He would teach me about forgiveness in the days ahead I didn't know, but tonight's was good news enough.

When we bring our sins to Jesus, He not only forgives them He makes them as if they had never been.[2]

Corrie ten Boon is not the only one who has wrestled with forgiveness. I think we all do—I know I have. When I went through one of the most difficult times of my life, I had to make the choice to forgive. I had to forgive Paul. This came so easy, as I saw his repentance not only toward God but toward me, his children, friends and the family of God. However, my battle with forgiveness was toward friends who chose to condemn rather than restore; those who had been so close to us for years and chose to shun me and the children because of Paul's sin. This was so hard. My children couldn't understand why they were being penalized. They hadn't done anything. They couldn't understand why my friends didn't call me to encourage me and speak words of hope and kindness. Needless to say, my children had their own battle with forgiveness, but they had to battle this by themselves.

I learned a lot about myself during this time, but one of the biggest things I learned is that it's easier to forgive a stranger than a friend. Before Paul and I walked this path, I would have been one of the first to condemn and not have anything to do with that person who "sinned." After all, I didn't want to be associated with a sinner like that. It grieves my heart to even write about my wicked behavior during this time, but I am so thankful that God forgives and restores and doesn't remind us of our past. I am so grateful for the gift of grace and mercy.

The atrocities that Corrie experienced in the death camps including the death of her father and Betsy, seemed unforgettable and unforgiveable. Anyone hearing her story would naturally sympathize with her struggle. But, God wants more than sympathy, He wants us to be merciful and give grace to others.

Our natural bend toward mere justice makes us stratify our sins and calculate our motivation for them. We consider one sin small and inconsequential, another large and if we ourselves could not commit that sin, we find it impossible to reconcile how another person could do this or that. But God knows what propels the motivations of what we do or don't do. Only He can see clearly the heart of each person.

The sins that lay at the foot of the cross are big or small, but His blood covers them all. Beside Jesus, a murderer and a thief were crucified. We don't know what was stolen or who was killed or why. The scripture does not say that one sin was worse than the other. We do know with certainty that what brought the thief on the cross beside Jesus into the Kingdom was his desperate faith ("Jesus, remember me when you come into your kingdom") and God's unfailing mercy ("I assure you today you will be with me in paradise"). God has shown His mercy to us. Do we have the faith to believe and to show that mercy to others?

> *If you forgive those who sin against you, your heavenly Father will forgive you. But if you refuse to forgive others, your Father will not forgive your sins* (Matthew 5:14-15 NLT).

PROMISES TO MEMORIZE OR MEDITATE UPON

> *Therefore, if any man be in Christ, he is a new creature: old things are passed away; behold, all things are become new. And all things are of God, who hath reconciled us to himself by Jesus Christ, and hath given to us the ministry of reconciliation; to wit, that God was in Christ, reconciling the world*

unto himself, not imputing their trespasses unto them; and hath committed unto us the word of reconciliation (2 Corinthians 5:17-19 KJV).

For thou, Lord, art good, and ready to forgive... (Psalm 86:5 KJV).

But with you there is forgiveness, that you may be feared (Psalm 130:4 ESV).

In whom we have redemption, the forgiveness of sins (Colossians 1:14 ESV).

Be kind and compassionate to one another, forgiving each other, just as in Christ God forgave you (Ephesians 4:32 NIV).

Do not judge, and you will not be judged. Do not condemn, and you will not be condemned. Forgive, and you will be forgiven (Luke 6:37 NIV).

And when you stand praying, if you hold anything against anyone, forgive them, so that your Father in heaven may forgive you your sins (Mark 11:25 NIV)

For the Lord your God is gracious and compassionate. He will not turn his face from you if you return to him (2 Chronicles 30:9 NIV).

Brethren, I do not count myself to have apprehended; but one thing I do, forgetting those things which are behind and reaching forward to those things which are ahead, I press toward the goal for the prize of the upward call of God in Christ Jesus (Philippians 3:13-14 NKJV).

Prayer

Thank You, thank You, thank You, Father, for Your forgiveness to me a sinner saved by grace. Thank You for giving me the grace to forgive others. Lord, show me if there is anyone I haven't forgiven. I want to have a clean heart before You. "Search me, O God, and know my heart: try me, and know my thoughts: And see if there be any wicked way in me, and lead me in the way everlasting" (Psalm 139:23-24 KJV). Amen.

What promise has God given to you today?

BONNIE JOHNSON

In all thy ways acknowledge him and he shall direct thy paths (Proverbs 3:6 KJV).

I woke up with that verse running through my head this morning and it made me think of all the times my parents repeated that verse to me and many others. We had a rule in our home that we never left the dinner table without our dad reading a chapter from the Bible and all of us kids had to pick out a verse to memorize for the next night. It is amazing how much you can remember when you are competing against your siblings. This whole process was one of the greatest gifts our parents could have given us. By the time my mom turned eighty-six, she had memorized two hundred and twenty poems and Bible verses.

I've used the provided verse many times as a parent or grandparent. When approached by one of my children or grandchildren with a problem or difficult situation, my worldly view of a proposed solution will sometimes change after I pray and ponder what my response or advice should be. In my mind, I can still see my parents praying together nightly; I have vivid memories of them kneeling together side by side acknowledging the great things that He has provided them, including their children, even though many times we didn't deserve such praise.

Noella Olynyk

Trust in the Lord with all your heart and lean not on your own understanding; in all your ways submit to him, and he will make your paths straight (Proverbs 3:5-6 NIV).

There is so much peace knowing that He is in control when our human understanding is exhausted. Control what you can: your attitude and actions. Other than that, we could never possibly comprehend the bigger picture that our Savior has in store for us. So, we must trust and rest in the peace that He is fully in control and even when I submit my perfect agenda. He has such a clearer picture than I do. Suffering, rejoicing, aching, thriving, no matter what. He's got this.

This promise seems to be one of the most "held-on" promises. I put these promises about God directing our paths here because I know He is faithful to "direct" and "guide" us into forgiveness. Let It Go! If we don't, we are the ones who suffer and are in bondage. We are the ones in prison.

ENDNOTES

1. Charles Spurgeon, *Treasury of David, Psalm 130.* https://archive.spurgeon.org/treasury/ps130.php; accessed November 8, 2021.

2. Corrie ten Boom, *The Hiding Place, 35th Anniversary Edition* (Grand Rapids, MI: Chosen, 1971), 200-218.

Chapter 4

HUSBANDS: A BLESSING FROM GOD

In the same way, you wives, be submissive to your own husbands [subordinate, not as inferior, but out of respect for the responsibilities entrusted to husbands and their accountability to God, and so partnering with them] so that even if some do not obey the word [of God], they may be won over [to Christ] without discussion by the godly lives of their wives, when they see your modest and respectful behavior [together with your devotion and appreciation—love your husband, encourage him, and enjoy him as a blessing from God]. Your adornment must not be merely external—with interweaving and elaborate knotting of the hair, and wearing gold jewelry, or [being superficially preoccupied with] dressing in expensive clothes; but let it be [the inner beauty of] the hidden person of the heart, with the imperishable quality

*and unfading charm of a gentle and peaceful spirit,
[one that is calm and self-controlled, not overanx-
ious, but serene and spiritually mature] which is
very precious in the sight of God.*

—1 PETER 3:1-4 AMP

God's promise is that our husbands will be won over to Christ and transformed as they see our godly lives and our honor and respect toward them. In short, God will do the changing! I know! We think we can do a better job of changing our husbands than God. But all we have to do is consider what has been accomplished with our ways of trying to change him. How does God change us? He works through our daily circumstances. He uses the difficulties of the here and now to transform us...yes, both husband and wife.

Listen dear friend, you are a sinner married to a sinner. I know when we are standing at the altar, we think we're marrying the perfect man. However, it didn't take us long to realize those expectations we had about our husband are unrealistic! In *Sacred Marriage*, Gary Thomas asks a question: "What if God designed marriage to make us holy more than to make us happy?" That's a very good question. I'm not saying you can't be happy in your marriage. I believe happiness, like love, is a choice. But God uses the everyday happenings in our lives to make us more like Christ. And, it seems God uses our husbands to transform us more than anyone on this earth. Paul, my hubby, uses the sandpaper illustration. We are each other's heavenly sandpaper to sand off everything that doesn't glorify God. It's painful, at times, but it is necessary.

What is marriage about? Is it having a gorgeous wedding? Is it having a beautiful home and adorable children? Is it expensive cars and jewelry? No! Even though there's nothing wrong with these things, marriage is about persevering through difficult times: hospital stays and paying bills, sick children and losing jobs, loss of loved ones, children going astray, debilitating illness, working through hard times and disagreements and struggles, sometimes working long hours. It's keeping faith and staying together through thick and thin.

I'm sure you read the part in the scripture where it says, "love your husband, encourage him, and enjoy him as a blessing from God." How many of you rolled your eyes when you read that part? A blessing? Please! Yes, my dear friend, a blessing. Sometimes we are so busy finding the "wrong" about our hubbies that we can't concentrate on the "good." With the same amount of passion, we want our husbands to love us in the same way we should respect, honor, cherish, submit and love our husbands. You may say, I don't love him anymore. It's not that you've fallen out of love, but could it be that you are unwilling to repent and get your heart right with God and obey God's Word? Love is a choice not an emotion. I read a statement that said emotions are a terrible master but a good servant. I know this isn't popular, but it's true.

What does it mean when it says "In the same way"? What way? In 1 Peter 2, Christ is our example of how we should live.

We are told how to live before the world, how to be submissive to our government, and how to submit to those we serve and those for whom we work. Then, we read in the "same way" or "likewise" be submissive to your own husbands.... Is this an easy thing to do? It all depends on who you want to please and if you want God's blessing.

In the garden, the serpent asked Eve if God really said she shouldn't eat from every tree. She answered him, "We can eat from every tree except the one in the middle of the garden, lest we die." Then the serpent went on to say, "You won't really die. God knows you will be like Him knowing good from evil, that's why He doesn't want you to have that fruit." I believe the enemy is speaking to us today, "Does God really expect you to be in submission to your husband? You have the right to be your own boss and be independent of God and man. Do your own thing! Does He really expect you to obey His word? This isn't your mother's generation!" (Genesis 3). Now, these are not the exact words, but it is the same temptation; be your own god! Live your life the way you want to live it. Leave God out!

I wrote a lot about submission in my book *Priceless*, so I encourage you to read the last chapter entitled, I'm Not Your Concubine. I explained submission very thoroughly in this chapter. Submission is not a bad word. It's obeying God's word, but it is also an attitude of the heart. It's a choice we make.

John Piper, in his book *Desiring God,* gives an example of his wife, Noel, submitting to him.

> Submission is an inclination of the will to say yes to
> the husband's leadership and a disposition of the spirit

to support his initiatives. The reason I say it's a disposition and an inclination is that there will be times when the most submissive wives will hesitate at a husband's decision. It may look unwise to her. Suppose it's Noël and I. I am about to decide something foolish for the family. At that moment Noël could express her submission something like this: "Johnny, I know you've thought a lot about this, and I love it when you take the initiative to plan for us and take the responsibility like this, but I really don't have peace about this decision and I think we need to talk about it some more. Could we? Maybe tonight sometime?"

When I read John's example of Noel's submission, I would be amiss not to see that it looks very much like being considerate and supportive, being gentle and kind and making him feel safe to admit if he has made a mistake, and expressing her appreciation of his efforts at loving, leading, and caring for his family. The ultimate reassurance would be if this plan actually needs to be shelved, Noel would show her faith in her husband by asking him if there is an alternate plan he thinks would work. Perhaps she would express her gratitude for him being flexible and considerate of her concerns.

We are not inferior to our husbands. We are completely equal and have the same value as our husbands, but God has put the husband as the head (authority) because God is a God of order not chaos (Ephesians 5:2-25).

Husbands have a huge responsibility entrusted to them by God. They are accountable to Him. God set the husband in authority over the family as protection. A husband is not to be a tyrant or to demand obedience. A caring husband will not lord over his wife. As you continue to read in the following verses in 1 Peter, you will see the responsibilities of a husband. His is to love her as Christ loves the church. He is to value her and honor her and know how precious she is, not only to him but to the Lord. An understanding husband realizes he and his wife are heirs together in the grace of life, or we can say, heirs together in the joy or pleasure of life. However, a wife cannot make her husband obey what God tells him, but she can obey how God has instructed her to behave.

I encourage ladies NOT to preach to their husband. Not to nag him about his lack of spiritual growth. Not to act superior in her spiritual life. Not to berate him. Not to quote scripture to him. But, as the scripture says, live a godly life in front of him. Love him. Encourage him. Respect him. Let him see your love for Jesus and your desire to please Him.

It seems so easy to show compassion and understanding to friends who are going through rebellion. We will share the love of Jesus with them, and we are so patient, kind and understanding with them. However, when it comes to our husband, we allow all the frustration and annoyance we've gathered over the years to overrule God's Word.

When we made a commitment to our spouse at the altar, what did that mean...as a Christian? In Ephesians 5 we read: *"But the fruit of the Spirit is love, joy, peace, longsuffering, kindness, goodness, faithfulness, meekness, self-control; against such there is no law."* When we say "I love you" to our spouse, what does that look like? Does it mean getting our own way, or should we prefer others before ourselves? Could it mean keeping a clean house rather than sitting all day on our "backside" (I could use another word, but I'm being kind) watching television, reading a book, or shopping with a friend? Could it be really listening to him after a long day of work? Could it be opting for the restaurant he enjoys rather than the one we always want to go to, and pouting if we don't get our way? Could it be putting down the book and paying attention to him...putting our phone away? There are so many ways to say I love you in our daily lives. If we are attentive, we will know exactly what we can do to show our love.

Joy is a way to show love. Does your husband see you as a cheerful and joyful person? Do you have a grateful heart, or do you murmur and complain? Are you thankful for your marriage even though it is nowhere near perfect? Do you look for good in him or concentrate on all the bad things?

Peace (quietness, rest)! It's amazing how much conflict there is in our daily lives: anger, impatience, resentment, and disappointment. So much of the time these attitudes are over little instances. Sin makes it easier to make war than to make peace. We bring up wrongs from years gone by rather than forgetting those things and making peace. We must learn to overlook all of those minor offenses. We must be quick to forgive. If we have truly forgiven a past wrong we won't bring it up again even in the worst fight. If we are going to serve in love, we must be committed to peace.

Kindness is another way to show our commitment to our spouse. In Proverbs 31 we read when the godly woman opens her mouth, it's with wisdom and kindness. Has this changed since we said "I do" at the altar? We should remember how kind we were when we were dating. How polite and patient we were with each other! After all, we were trying to win each other's affection and love. Let me ask a question. Would your spouse say you are kind, or would he say that you are critical? When Paul and I counsel, we never ask the husband how he treats his wife. We ask the wife how he treats her. And, of course, we never ask the wife how kind she is, we ask the husband. You see, we can lie to ourselves. We can be easily deceived. Plus, we can look in the mirror of God's Word and He will reveal our hearts and give us grace to repent. We should treat our spouse as kindly and more respectfully than we treat others.

When we serve our spouse in love, we will be *faithful* to the vows we repeated when we were at the altar pledging our loyalty to each other. Where does unfaithfulness begin? In our thoughts and desires. If we fantasize being with someone other than our spouse, this is unfaithfulness. Do our personal desires come before him? Have we allowed bitterness to invade our minds? Are we too busy to be attentive to our spouse? Are we unwilling to forgive?

When our spouse says something hurtful, do we respond with *gentleness* or do we react in anger? One of the greatest truths in God's Word is in Proverbs (15:1), which tells us that when we answer with a soft answer (voice and attitude) instead of a harsh voice, it will put out the fire that will stir if answered with a harsh answer. I read a quote years ago that said, "90 percent of the friction of everyday life is started with the wrong tone of voice." How true this is! We can say, "I'm really sorry!" Or we can scream out, "I SAID I WAS SORRY!" I know we can all identify with both responses. Let's be gentle, not only with friends, but especially with our husbands.

Gratefulness is a wonderful way to show love to our husbands. It's amazing what gratitude can do for a marriage. When a spouse is thankful, and actually verbalizes this, it can do wonders for a marriage. When a wife lets her hubby know how much she appreciates his hard work and has a desire to take care of his family, this motivates him to work even harder. This encourages him! This blesses him. He knows what he is doing isn't in vain. He feels appreciated. He feels validated. However, if a wife is constantly discontent and complaining or she shows dissatisfaction with what her husband provides, this is debilitating, and he will be discouraged. God's Word says that God's goodness is what leads a person to repentance. Do you want your husband to change? Well, stop berating him and start praising him. He may decide to live up to your praise.

> It is painful when you have been hurt, but to lash back is never a step toward reconciliation. There may be no more needed character in marriage than self-control. It is the constant willingness to critique your thoughts, edit your words, and restrain your behavior out of love for your spouse and love for what is right. Self-control means you simply won't give yourself permission to get down and dirty. You will take the time that you need to be in a place where you can speak and act with love,

wisdom, grace, and gentleness and be committed to unity, understanding and peace.[1]

A very wise person once told me—and you may have already heard this—that hurt people hurt people and healed people heal people. Ask the Lord to give you eyes to see beyond the facade or exterior harshness of your husband. Ask the Lord to help you see the heart of your husband and what he might need. Ask the Lord to give you words that will be a healing agent in his life so that "...together *with your devotion and appreciation and encouragement, you love and enjoy him as a blessing from God."*

PROMISES TO MEMORIZE OR MEDITATE UPON

Love endures with patience and serenity, love is kind and thoughtful, and is not jealous or envious; love does not brag and is not proud or arrogant. It is not rude; it is not self-seeking; it is not provoked [nor overly sensitive and easily angered]; it does not consider a wrong endured. It does not rejoice at injustice but rejoices with the truth [when right and truth prevail]. Love bears all things [regardless of what comes], believes all things [looking for the best in each one], hopes all things [remaining steadfast during difficult times], endures all things [without weakening. Love never fails [it never fades nor ends]... (1 Corinthians 13:4-8 AMP).*

It is better to live in a corner of the housetop than in a house shared with a quarrelsome wife (Proverbs 21:9 ESV).

Who can find a virtuous wife? For her worth is far above rubies. The heart of her husband safely trusts her... (Proverbs 31:10-11 NKJV).

Beloved, let us love one another, for love is from God, and whoever loves has been born of God and knows God. Anyone who does not love does not know God, because God is love (1 John 4:7-8 ESV).

Wives, submit to your husbands, as is fitting in the Lord (Colossians 3:18 ESV).

Prayer

Father, I don't want to be one of those women whose husband wants to live on the rooftop because I'm so cantankerous. I want to have a kind and gentle spirit so that I will be a living testament to him. "Set a watch, O LORD, before my mouth; keep the door of my lips" (Psalm 141:3 KJV). Amen.

What promise has God given to you today?

SANDY HAWKINS

"For I know the plans I have for you," declares the Lord, "plans to prosper you and not to harm you, plans to give you hope and a future" (Jeremiah 29:11 NIV).

I love this verse because when I hear it, read it or speak it, I am immediately filled with hope. It has been one of my favorite "hope" scriptures for years. Just knowing that the Lord's plan is to prosper me and to give me hope and a future, always gives me strength to get through whatever the situation may be. A few years ago I received a crystal award plaque from a board I serve on; and when they contacted Bill and asked for a favorite scripture or quote of mine to engrave on the plaque, Bill gave them Jeremiah 29:11. Just this past January we had a family meeting to kick off 2020 and we decided we wanted to have a family scripture/promise for the year and we chose Jeremiah 29:11. It definitely is a meaningful promise to our family during such a time as this.

Jen Brown

> *Trust in the Lord with all your heart and lean not on your own understanding; in all your ways submit to him and he will make your paths straight* (Proverbs 3:6 NIV).

For as long as I can recall, this has been a verse and a promise from God that has provided me with some of the greatest peace. So many of us are guilty of trying to nail down and control everything around us—our husbands, our children, people we mentor, business results, you name it! When I sit and meditate on this word I am able to let go of the pressure to do things in my own strength and in my own timing. Patience is a virtue for a reason and my theme song should be "Let it Go!" I am constantly reminded of the goodness of God and the desire for Him to make our paths straight, to encourage and bless us and allow us to make the impact He needs us to make. It's so comforting knowing He is ultimately in control and truly wants the best for us in all things, even when it may not look, sound, or feel the way we picture.

ENDNOTE

1. Paul David Tripp, *What Did You Expect?* (Wheaton, IL: Crossway, 2010), 126.

Chapter 5

PEACE: GOD IS OUR SOURCE

Do not be anxious or worried about anything, but in everything [every circumstance and situation] by prayer and petition with thanksgiving, continue to make your [specific] requests known to God. And the peace of God [that peace which reassures the heart, that peace] which transcends all understanding, [that peace which] stands guard over your hearts and your minds in Christ Jesus [is yours].
—PHILIPPIANS 4:6-7 AMP

His promise is peace that passes all understanding when we obey His Word. God is not talking about worldly peace but a peace that only He can give.

There's an old hymn written in 1889 that speaks to my heart. I have sung this song for many years. What thrills my heart is that 100 years later, while going through a very trying time, I was singing this song of encouragement and promise; *peace, peace, His wonderful peace is flowing down from my Father.* If it's one thing we need daily, it's God's peace, and He promises this peace when we keep our hearts and minds focused on Him, because He alone is our source.

What is the difference between peace *with* God and the peace *of* God? Peace with God comes upon us at salvation. Peace with God means a restored relationship. I had peace *with* God the moment I put my faith and trust in Christ as my Lord and Savior in 1974. Nothing and no one can ever change that. I was born again into the family of God. Jesus is the Prince of Peace. The Holy Spirit brings peace.

One of the greatest joys in my life was when I was saved. I didn't change much on the outside, but the inside was completely renovated by God's transforming power. I immediately experienced His peace! This was something that alluded me all my religious years of growing up. Only God can work this miracle in a person's life.

On the other hand, peace of God is the assurance that I can trust God, that He is sovereign in my life in all circumstances and that His Spirit is inside of me compelling me toward Him. The peace of God is not just an emotion, but the Holy Spirit being active in my heart and the renewing of my mind. A friend of mine told me the following story. It is not some earth shattering miracle, just an account of how we experience God's peace in our everyday circumstances.

When I became a Christian, I was inexperienced with trusting God. I had not yet walked minute by minute aware of or experiencing His love and devotion. I had a key verse that I hung on to and repeated to myself about 500 times a day: *"Trust in the Lord with all your heart, and lean not on your own understanding; in all your ways acknowledge Him, and He shall direct your paths"* (Proverbs 3:5-6). I don't remember who gave that verse to me, but it became a part of me and held me fast as I began to experience the Lord working in my life.

Little by little, the Lord began to grow me up as I recognized His hand in my daily affairs. Sometimes what seemed like a sure train wreck ahead was a shift in direction or an unveiling of a problem in which I had no awareness. An example would be when I got a call that my mom had been rushed to the hospital because of seizures. Recently she had not been well, but for some reason an immediate peace flowed over me. I didn't know how or why, but I knew the Lord was in this situation. I actually started off to the hospital singing and thanking Him. At the end of the emergency, the doctor recognized that my mom had been over-medicated and was able to start her on a new and safe regimen. She regained a healthy equilibrium and was her old self. The Lord was in this situation. The Lord brought salvation out of a situation that looked dim on the face of it: *"All things work together for those who love God and are called according to His purpose"* (Romans 8:28). Now I had another scripture to say 500 times a day!

Sometimes my heart is troubled about certain situations that cause me not to have the peace of God. Worry is the opposite of peace. There is a strong correlation between choices and our peace. If we harbor unforgiveness in our heart or are filled with anger; if we have hatred toward anyone, we can certainly obliterate the peace of God. Therefore, it is so important to let the peace of God rule (be the umpire) in our hearts (Colossians 3:15-16).

God's promise of peace doesn't depend on circumstances in our world. What the world describes as peace—circumstances, wealth, prosperity, popularity is always fluctuating and isn't true peace. It's built on a weak foundation which denies the truth of God's Word. God's peace is everlasting. Because we have been reconciled to God in Christ, even if our circumstances are challenging, we are promised the blessing of His peace in our daily lives. His peace is not circumstantial; it depends on us trusting in Him.

When our oldest son, Paul Edward, was nine years old, he started having severe pain in different areas of his body. One day I could touch his legs and he would scream. The next day the pain had moved to his abdomen or arms. I had taken him to a number of doctors who took all of 5 minutes to examine him and just guessed what was wrong. Paul was on the road in evangelism at this time, so I was really facing this alone. I was desperate for God to give me direction. I called my mother-in-law for some answers. She told me to have the doctors do a certain test to determine if he had rheumatic fever. She knew the symptoms because Paul Sr. had suffered with this when he was young. Sure enough, I had an answer. Finally, a young doctor took time to listen to Paul Edward's heartbeat, and immediately put him in the hospital. As I look back at this situation, I know God was giving me that "peace that passes all understanding."

I was a very young Christian at this time, so all I knew to do was "cry to the Lord." Even in the midst of a suffering child, the Lord had stilled my heart—I had peace. The words of Thomas Watson, never seemed more true to me:

> If God be our God, He will give us peace in trouble.
> When there is a storm without, He will make peace
> within. The world can create trouble in peace, but
> God can create peace in trouble.
>
> —THOMAS WATSON

As a Christian, you do not have to live a life of aggravation and frustration. You have God's Spirit living inside of you. He will empower you to have the peace that is promised as you walk with Him. As the scripture says in Philippians 4, when we keep our hearts and minds on godly things, when we meditate on His word, the God of peace will be with us. This is His promise to us.

There are 365 promises of God's peace in the Bible, one for each day of the year. We will have His peace when we take His promises into our lives and believe.

> *Finally, believers, whatever is true, whatever is*
> *honorable and worthy of respect, whatever is right*
> *and confirmed by God's word, whatever is pure and*
> *wholesome, whatever is lovely and brings peace,*
> *whatever is admirable and of good repute; if there is*
> *any excellence, if there is anything worthy of praise,*
> *think continually on these things [center your mind*
> *on them, and implant them in your heart]. The*

things which you have learned and received and heard and seen in me, practice these things [in daily life], and the God [who is the source] of peace and well-being will be with you (Philippians 4:8-9 AMP).

PROMISES TO MEMORIZE OR MEDITATE UPON

For He Himself is our peace, who has made both one, and has broken down the middle wall of separation (Ephesians 2:14 NKJV).

I will hear what God the Lord will speak, for He will speak peace to His people and to His saints; but let them not turn back to folly (Psalm 85:8 NKJV).

Peace I leave with you, My peace I give to you; not as the world gives do I give to you. Let not your heart be troubled, neither let it be afraid (John 14:27 NKJV).

You will keep him in perfect peace, whose mind is stayed on You, because he trusts in You (Isaiah 26:3 NKJV).

But the fruit of the Spirit is love, joy, peace, patience, kindness, goodness, faithfulness, gentleness, self-control; against such things there is no law (Galatians 5:22-23 NASB).

Prayer

Lord, thank You for Your peace that passes my understanding. Thank You, that in the middle of a storm, when everything seems out of control,

You give me Your peace. Help me to keep my mind on You. Don't let my mind go to places that drag me down and defeat me. I want to think of those things that are pleasing to You. Amen.

What promise has God given to you today?

KIMBERLY EATON

Be still, and know that I am God: I will be exalted among the heathen, I will be exalted in the earth. The Lord of hosts is with us; the God of Jacob is our refuge. Selah (Psalm 46:10-11 KJV).

If you look around my home, I probably have four or five pictures or signs in my home with the scripture "Be still." I specifically remember 17 years ago, when we were living in a junkie rental house, life was very interesting at the time. We were building our business, we had three small kids, Tracey was a full-time stockbroker, and the market crashed a few years earlier. Our life seemed to be going backwards in so many ways and I was very, very discouraged. I don't know where I heard it but I specifically remember one night painting with a paintbrush over our bed, "Be still." It's one of those things that helps me to exhale and keep things in perspective and not react or respond too quickly to overwhelming emotions...and remind myself that God truly is in control at the right place at the right time.

ANN GOLDEN

Whatever you ask in My name, that will I do, so that the Father may be glorified in the Son. If you ask anything in My name, I will do it (John 14:13-14 NKJV).

This verse has been my favorite for years. Not all things are good, but God takes the all and works it for our good and His glory. He has proven this to me so many times.

THERESA ATTALAH

Finally, brethren, whatsoever things are true, whatsoever things are honest, whatsoever things are just, whatsoever things are pure, whatsoever things are lovely, whatsoever things are of good report; if there be any virtue, and if there be any praise, think on these things (Philippians 4:8 KJV).

One of my favorite Bible verses is Philippians 4:6-8. I love these promises that the Lord hears my prayers, and if I trust in Him and keep my thoughts purely focused on Him, then all the "what if's" in life are crushed. There are many things in this life that we can worry about—children, finances, health, the future, and on and on. If I present my worries and give them to the Lord, I can trust that He hears my prayers and will cover all those precious people and things with His loving arms. One of my favorite things to do is write out my prayer requests and place them on a tall shelf in my closet as if I am releasing those worries, fears etc., to the Lord for Him to handle them. I can then focus on the things that are true, noble, pure, lovely, admirable, excellent or praiseworthy!

BARBARA MORALES

Trust in the Lord with all your heart, and lean not on your own understanding; in all your ways submit to Him, and He shall direct your paths (Proverbs 3:5-6).

Many years ago at church I received my program for that Sunday's service and that scripture was printed on my program. I looked at my husband's and his program did not have it, then I asked others and their's did not have it either. So, I felt it was God's personal message to me. It became my favorite scripture from that moment on.

Chapter 6

PLANTING GOOD
SEED; REAPING LIFE

Let us not grow weary or become discouraged in doing good, for at the proper time we will reap, if we do not give in. So then, while we [as individual believers] have the opportunity, let us do good to all people [not only being helpful, but also doing that which promotes their spiritual well-being], and especially [be a blessing] to those of the household of faith (born-again believers).

—GALATIANS 6:9-10 AMP

Are you praying for someone you love to come to Christ? Are you believing someone you love will be healed, set free from an addictive situation, families restored, children returning home?

Don't give up! Continue to pray and believe God will work a miracle. Don't be weary! God may not answer the way we want Him to answer, but He will answer according to His will. He will give grace no matter the outcome.

Most of us may not hear or use the words reaping and sowing much outside of scripture or planting. The Bible uses the idea of sowing as a metaphor of what we invest in our lives and the lives of those around us. It's very simple: we plant good seed, we harvest good fruit; we plant bad seeds, we harvest no fruit or poor fruit. Likewise, if we plant apple seeds we won't get watermelons. Whatever seeds you plant and water and fertilize will grow and thrive.

In God's Word, He tells us He will not be mocked—you can't fool Him—He sees the truth and He knows you. Whatever a man sows, that is what he will reap. It amazes me that people blame God when bad things come their way even though they are just suffering the consequences of their choices, good or bad! When we sow to our sinful nature, we are going to reap destruction: adultery, fornication, uncleanness, lewdness, idolatry, sorcery, hatred, contentions, jealousies, outbursts of wrath, selfish ambitions, dissensions, heresies, envy, murders, drunkenness, revelries, and the like. When we sow in the spirit: love, joy, peace, longsuffering, kindness, goodness, faithfulness, gentleness, self-control, we will reap the same (Galatians 5).

I'm a big plant lover. I love my garden. When I plant a tomato plant, I fully expect to get tomatoes. When I plant peppers, I get the same kind of peppers I planted. What I sow, I will reap. I don't expect figs from my peach tree or blackberries from my pecan trees. So, what I sow in the ground is what I will reap when harvest time comes. This truth never changes.

The metaphor of planting seeds and reaping engulfs our lives. We live in an area where there are cotton, corn, milo, and rice fields. As I drive by these fields, I can tell if the farmers were generous or stingy with the seeds when they planted their fields. There's one field I pass by that has stalks of corn four or five feet apart. It looks terrible. Then, I pass by many fields that are generously seeded. Who do you think will get the better harvest? Of course, the ones who planted generously. It's the same with our lives. If we sow generously in love, we will reap much love. If we sow generously in giving, we will reap generously. If we sow generously in encouragement, we will reap encouragement. You get the message! So, sow generously! Be a cheerful giver!

I believe one of the best examples I can use for reaping what we sow is my husband. He is the greatest at edifying and encouraging people. He is always speaking words that edify and he knows how to make people feel great about themselves. For years he has done this with me, our children and their spouses, our grandchildren and their spouses, our great grandchildren, and our friends. He seems to know the right words that will make everyone's day. I'm not saying he doesn't sometimes do the opposite when he's upset, but most of the time, he is full of kind, encouraging, uplifting and edifying words. So, because of his discipline in this area, he continually gets this returned to him in abundance.

Generosity of life in every area will bring generosity to our lives. Sowing and reaping is one of the most profound principles in life. In Paul's book, *What You Seed is What You Get,* are the biblical principles for a life of biblical prosperity. Use generous words; be charitable with your possessions and your time. My encouragement to you today is to become a generous life-giver.

PROMISES TO MEMORIZE OR MEDITATE UPON

...He who sows sparingly will also reap sparingly, and he who sows bountifully will also reap bountifully (2 Corinthians 9:6 NKJV).

Now may He who supplies seed to the sower, and bread for food, supply and multiply the seed you have sown and increase the fruits of your righteousness, while you are enriched in everything for all liberality, which causes thanksgiving through us to God (2 Corinthians 9:10-11 NKJV).

Give, and it will be given to you: good measure, pressed down, shaken together, and running over will be put into your bosom. For with the same measure that you use, it will be measured back to you (Luke 6:38 NKJV).

There is the one who [generously] scatters [abroad], and yet increases all the more; and there is the one who withholds what is justly due, but it results only in want and poverty. The generous man [is a source of blessing and] shall be prosperous and enriched, and he who waters will himself be watered [reaping the generosity he has sown] (Proverbs 11:24-25 AMP).

Judge not, and ye shall not be judged: condemn not, and ye shall not be condemned: forgive, and ye shall be forgiven (Luke 6:37 KJV).

He who is gracious and lends a hand to the poor lends to the LORD, and the LORD will repay him for his good deed (Proverbs 19:17 AMP).

Prayer

Father, I want to be a gracious giver in every area of my life. I want to sow love because You are love. I want to sow kindness. I want to sow encouragement. I want to sow abundantly in every area of my life. Teach me Your ways! Amen.

What promise has God given to you today?

BRILEY NGUYEN

"For I know the plans I have for you," says the Lord. *"They are plans for good and not for disaster, to give you a future and a hope"* (Jeremiah 29:11 NLT). God can be trusted—*"Let us hold tightly without wavering to the hope we affirm, for God can be trusted to keep his promise"* (Hebrews 10:23 NLT).

When crisis has come up in my life or things have seemed like they were never going to get better or wouldn't work out, remembering that God has my very best at heart has always helped me so much. He wants hope for my future and then I can always trust Him. That has helped me through so many times of discouragement, doubt or fear in my life. It's always been a comfort and assurance that ultimately everything is going to be okay. Beauty comes from the ashes and sometimes crisis is the way to restoration.

THERESA DANZIK

> *If you remain in me and my word remains in you, ask what you wish and it will done for you. This is to my Father's glory that you bear much fruit, showing yourself to be my disciples* (John 15:7-8 NIV).

Waiting on the Lord for Him to bring me my husband, God had called me to go Diamond as a single. It took 3 years to go Diamond 1991-1994. Two years later, in 1996, I connected with Howie at the Grand Plaza Hotel at Amway's Diamond Convention. We got married on April 13, 1997. Our wedding theme—Days of Heaven Upon the Earth (Deut. 11:21).

We did not know each other back then but we both had accepted Christ on the same date, April 14th, 1991. I came to the Lord on a beach in Hawaii and Howie was at a Spring Leadership Sunday morning service with Terry and Linda Felber!

I love this verse that Theresa has stood on. She knew in her heart that God would hear her prayer and answer. She remained steadfast in her belief in God, without a doubt, He has given her much fruit for her labor, and a godly husband.

ANDREA PHILLIPS

> *Behold, I have given you authority to tread on serpents and scorpions, and over all the power of*

the enemy, and nothing shall hurt you (Luke 10:19 ESV)

God gave me this verse to remind me His power is greater, and He has given me the authority over evil, to promise me His divine protection over any circumstance, fear, or anxiety.

Chapter 7

CHILDREN: GOD IS SOVEREIGN OVER THEM

*Train up a child in the way he should go: and when
he is old, he will not depart from it.*
—PROVERBS 22:6 KJV

As I read the Old Testament in 1st and 2nd Kings, I'm amazed at the kings who ruled. Some were wicked. Some were godly. The wicked did what was evil in the sight of God; they set up idols in the temple and worshiped Baal, a false god. Then a son or grandson would come along and take the throne and remove the idols and worship the true and living God. I often wonder what causes those, who apparently were raised to honor God, to become ones who despise God and turn their backs on what they were taught. Or, what causes those who were raised by ungodly parents to turn their hearts to the Lord and worship Him.

I see this today in families. Parents who love Jesus raise their children in church, love their children, teach them the right way to go, yet they head off in the wrong direction. Then I've known those children who were raised in a godless home rise and be a beacon of light for the Lord. Baffling, unless we realize that our God is sovereign and is ruling and reigning.

James Robison has been a minister of the gospel for many years. He has a tremendous testimony of someone who was fatherless, abused, insecure, shy, and socially awkward, yet God raised him up to be one of the most influential men of our day.

James is a product of rape. His mother, who was 40 years old at the time of his birth, almost aborted him. Yet, God had other plans. His mother put an ad in the newspaper which read "WANTED loving Christian couple to raise newborn boy. References required." A Christian couple, a pastor and his wife, answered the ad. They raised him until he was five years old. His birth mother decided she wanted him back and took him from the only secure and loving home he knew. He spent the next 10 years in poverty and hunger, moving from town to town. His biological dad came back into his life when James was 15 years old. James had hopes that this would be a new beginning. However, his dad had not changed. He was an abusive alcoholic. James got back in touch with the couple who had raised him until he was five years old. There he gave his heart to the Lord and surrendered to preach. He is the founder of Life Outreach Today.

Now, here is a great example of someone who could have hated the world and everyone in it. He could have felt sorry for himself. He could have rebelled against God for the way he was treated by his real parents. Yet, he gave his heart to the Lord and became a minister of grace and mercy for the hurting.

> If your conscience is clear before the Lord, we'd encourage you to take heart and stop blaming yourself for the mistakes of your children. You can't make their decisions for them or control their relationship with God. If they have rebelled against you and rejected your faith in spite of your best efforts to defuse their hostile attitude and behavior, try to take some comfort in the thought that you've been faithful to your responsibilities and obligations as a parent. Bear in mind, too, that the final chapter of their story has yet to be written. God will use their youthful errors to teach them valuable lessons and bring them at last to a place of humility and repentance. This is evident from the examples of many biblical characters such as Jacob (deceiver), Joseph's brothers, and Jonah. Remember the exact words in which Proverbs 22:6 expresses its "statement of probability:" *"When he is old, he will not depart from it."* Isn't this how God used and is using everything we experience in life to train us?[1]

Don't give up on your children. Pray without ceasing. You never know when or how God will bring them back to Himself.

Be patient! Be loving! Be long suffering! Hasn't God been this way with us?

I'm including a prayer by Dudley and Betsy Hall that they prayed every day when their son, David, decided he didn't believe anything he had been taught. David was sure what his mom and dad believed was "narrow-minded, exclusive, and based on religious prejudice". I'm sure there are no words to express the pain and sorrow, and blaming oneself, that comes when a child you raised and desperately love tells you he/she is defecting from the Christian faith.

Dudley and Betsy held on to the passage of scripture where Jesus gave the parable about the unjust judge in Luke 18. I understand their persistence in praying. Oh, Lord, give us a heart to believe like this widow woman who went continually before the unjust judge until he finally gave in so she would stop bothering him. Don't give up! Pray! Pray! Pray!

> Dear Father, I know You're not an unjust judge and that I do not have to pester You into hearing me. I am one of your chosen ones. I thank You for choosing me to be Your son and Your representative on the earth. I have been the victim of an assault by an adversary who is seeking to steal my son and Yours. I am asking that You would intervene quickly and grant justice in this case. I am praying that You will put Your laws into his mind and into his heart, replacing the deception that has entered there. I am praying that You will be his God and defend him against all others who are trying to replace

You. I am asking You to make him know You by special revelation of Yourself, and I am praying that You would forgive his wickedness and remember his sins no more. And Father, I realize that Your "quickly" and my "quickly" may not mean the same thing, but I can only operate on the time that I live in, and it is short. So, I am asking You to do this today, and I believe that You shall. And I am asking that if You can't do it today, do it tomorrow. In Jesus' name, Amen.[2]

After two years of being faithful to pray this prayer daily, David returned home to his parents. He serves in ministry with his dad today. Hallelujah! NEVER GIVE UP!

There's a verse in Isaiah 42:3 that is a great reminder of God's love for His children: "*A bruised reed he will not break, and a faintly burning wick he will not quench.*" What a great promise of God's loving and tender care for us as His children! God is loving and tender toward our children too.

I have tomato plants that I take great care of, especially when they have tomatoes on them. When the vine gets very heavy with fruit, it sometimes breaks, but not completely severed from the plant. I don't rip the broken part off the vine. I gently lift it up and tie it to a stake so it continues to get life from the vine. This is the way our heavenly Father treats us when we are broken and bruised in this life. He is the God who restores, strengthens, and comforts. When there's no one to comfort or encourage you, He is always present. When you belong to Him, you are never alone.

I'm also a candle lover. I have a few in every room in our house, at the bay house, and at the condo in North Carolina. You can never have enough candles! Some of the candles don't burn as well as other candles. The wick in some candles is very touchy! But when a wick is not burning right, I don't toss the candle away. After all, it's still giving light and burning a little. It still has "life" in it. God doesn't throw us away or snuff out our lives because we aren't living the way we should, doing what we should. No, He is a tender High Priest who is touched by the feeling of our infirmities...our weaknesses, and He offers mercy and grace in our time of need. We can run into His arms and find comfort. He loves us with an unfailing love. His love is unconditional. He works in our lives to bring us back to shining bright and beautiful.

So, how do we pray for our children if they decide to turn aside from God and His truth? We do like Dudley and Betsy did, continue to pray and believe God will bring them back into the fold. Just like sheep are cared for and brought back into the fold, God will do this for us (Isaiah 53:6).

As parents we've all made mistakes. Once we've acknowledged those to a wayward child and asked forgiveness, we just keep on believing God on their behalf. One day those lost sheep will come home—a good shepherd guiding them all the way.

Paul and I were parked beside a church, when we lived in our bus, and I looked out of the window and saw an empty playground with swings being moved by the wind. My mind went back to when our children were young. I was sad for a while, but as I began to think about their futures, I was filled with praise and thanksgiving to our Lord for allowing us to have them for a few years. God had given them each a wonderful spouse. Grandchildren were on the way! The Lord had showed us that His Spirit was in them holding and guiding and caring tenderly for them. I wrote...

I see empty swings on the playground
rocking back and forth
Empty slides and seesaws
and an empty soldier's fort.
There's no one running through the house
or yelling down the hall
No one with a crayon
marking up the bedroom wall.
Where are all my children now?
They're all grown up and gone
God has called them all to leave this place
They once called home.
Empty swings and silent halls,
They don't make me sad.
My heart is full of gratitude
For the sovereign God they had.
Where are all my children now?
They have children of their own.
And their children that are grown
Have children of their own.
I see them playing with their toys

This fills my heart with so much joy,
They are running in the hall
Coloring on the bedroom wall
I love that I have children in my house, once again.
BILIE KAYE TSIKA. 1991

PROMISES TO MEMORIZE

He will feed His flock like a shepherd: He will gather the lambs with His arm, and carry them in His bosom, and gently lead those who are with young (Isaiah 40:11 NKJV).

You will keep in perfect peace those whose minds are steadfast, because they trust in you. Trust in the Lord forever, for the Lord, the Lord himself, is the Rock eternal (Isaiah 26:3-4 NIV).

Come to me, all you who are weary and burdened, and I will give you rest. Take my yoke upon you and learn from me, for I am gentle and humble in heart, and you will find rest for your souls. For my yoke is easy and my burden is light (Matthew 11:28-30 NIV).

I have said these things to you, that in me you may have peace. In the world you will have tribulation. But take heart; I have overcome the world (John 16:33 ESV).

Pray without ceasing (1 Thessalonians 5:17 NKJV).

Prayer

Lord, thank You for godly parents and grandparents who stand on Your Word and believe You will do exactly what You promised. Our children may stray, but You will bring them back to You. Continue to work in my heart to hold on to the promise You gave. Let me not give up or get weary in praying for my children. Amen.

What promise has God given you today?

NICOLE ERICKSON

"For I know the plans I have for you," declares the Lord, "Plans to prosper you and not to harm you, plans to give you a hope and a future" (Jeremiah 29:11 NIV).

I've learned to trust the Lord through good times and bad a long time ago. This Bible verse has always brought me great comfort, knowing the Lord is in control, and He loves me. When I put my trust in Him, I always have hope for a better tomorrow, regardless of circumstances because, ultimately, He is in control of my future. Even through bad or extremely difficult times, the Lord will never leave me, and He STILL has plans to prosper me and not to allow any harm to have victory. My promise/ trust is to believe the Lord and know that He never lies, He always keeps His promises and has a great plan for my life. It gives me peace and joy, keeping my promise to trust Him completely.

LINDA FELBER

Promise #1: *"Be still and know that I am God"* (Ps. 46:10). That's the first scripture that comes to me when I'm facing challenges. That causes me to take a deep breath, and to calm down. It brings me peace and comfort!

Promise #2 *"Train up a child in the way he should go, and when he is old he will not depart from it"* (Prov. 22:6). We stand on that promise for our children, grandchildren, and great grandchildren.

I, too, have stood on this promise for my children. Did they make mistakes? Yes. Did they make wrong choices? Yes. Did they live an exemplary Christian life? No! Did they do things that grieved my heart? Yes. But God! He knew right where they were always and was NOT going to let them go. They belong to Him, so I had to trust that He would work in their hearts and bring them back to Himself.

Praise God for godly parents and grandparents who stand in the gap for their families. The enemy is out to kill, steal and destroy, but God will hear the cries of His children. Keep on praying and believing God!

ENDNOTES

1. *Focus on The Family,* "What Does 'Train Up a Child in the Way He Should God' Really Mean for Parents?" https://www.focusonthefamily.com/family-qa/ parent-disillusioned-by-train-up-a-child-in-the-way -he-should-go/; accessed November 8, 2021.

2. Dudley Hall, *Incense & Thunder, Experience Intimacy and Power with God through Prayer* (Sisters, OR: Multnomah, 1999), 233-234.

Chapter 8

HIS COMMANDMENTS: KEYS TO LIFE AND PEACE

My son, do not forget my law, but let your heart keep my commands; For length of days and long life and peace they will add to you. Let not mercy and truth forsake you; bind them around your neck, write them on the tablet of your heart, and so find favor and high esteem in the sight of God and man. Trust in the Lord with all your heart, and lean not on your own understanding; in all your ways acknowledge Him, And He shall direct your paths. Do not be wise in your own eyes fear the Lord and depart from evil. It will be health to your flesh, and strength to your bones. Honor the Lord with your possessions, and with the first fruits of all your increase; so your barns will be filled with plenty, and your vats will overflow with new wine.
— PROVERBS 3:1-10 NKJV

Remember, the commandments of the Lord have as much to do with the promises of God as with the demands of God, that we might have His wisdom. A long life is promised to those who keep His commands; esteem and favor in the sight of God and man is promised to those who are merciful and honest; the Lord promises direction and guidance if you keep your eyes on Him; health and vitality is promised if you honor Him; and plentiful provision is promised when you acknowledge everything comes from Him.

Proverbs is one of the wisdom books of the Old Testament. And, boy, do we need wisdom to walk through this world! Wisdom is spoken about in many chapters of this book. Why do we need godly wisdom? We need wisdom to become skillful in honoring our parents, raising children, being responsible with our finances, conducting our sexual lives, our work ethic, how to treat people (friends and enemies alike), how to take care of our bodies, and so much more. It covers every aspect of our lives. There's no other book in the Bible that gives more attention to these matters than the Proverbs.

As I read verse 1 of this promise in Proverbs, I'm reminded of Psalm 119. This chapter is all about God's laws, commandments, statues, testimonies, ways, word, judgments, and precepts. There are so many promises in this passage: long life, peace, health, strength, provisions, favor with God and man. What more could a person ask for? However, there's a condition to every promise. God never says just live the way we want to live, and we'll be blessed. He says, "Don't forget My law." There's always an "if" to every promise. If we give generously, we will get generously. If we show love, we will receive love. If we trust in the Lord, He will direct our paths. If we forgive, we will be forgiven.

There are laws in this universe; physical law is one, such as gravity. This law governs everything on this planet. We don't even think about this daily. We just accept that gravity is at work. In physics, gravity is the natural force that causes objects to fall toward the earth. No matter how much I try to understand, I can't even fathom how we can stand on the earth and not be thrown off as the earth spins at approximately 1,000 miles an hour or that it rushes around the sun at 67,000 miles an hour. Why aren't we thrown off when we are moving at this speed? Gravity! Science tries to explain that it just happened that way, but we know that God is the Creator of this universe and He set this up from the beginning (Genesis 1). His laws will never change.

The same goes for God's moral law. Christian or not, when you break this law, the result is exactly what God says. Why? Because God created the universe with humans to operate in a particular way. God's moral law is concerned with both the internal and external of man's life. An example of Old Testament law is don't commit adultery, but God's moral law (under grace) says if you even look at a woman/man to lust after her/him you have already committed adultery in your heart. Another example is:

> *You have heard that it was said, "You shall love your neighbor and hate your enemy." But I say to you, love your enemies, bless those who curse you, do good*

to those who hate you, and pray for those who spite-
fully use you and persecute you, that you may be sons
of your Father in heaven; for He makes His sun rise
on the evil and on the good, and sends rain on the
just and on the unjust (Matthew 5:43-45 NKJV).

So we see that grace is stricter than the law.

I encourage you to read the Proverbs every day. There are 31 chapters—one for each day of the month. So, if you read one chapter every day, you will read through Proverbs 12 times in a year. You will learn something new every day of every month because His Word is alive and fresh every morning (see Lamentations 3:22-23 NKJV).

I would also encourage you to read and meditate on Psalm 119. There are 176 verses which deal with God's commands (statues, law, testimonies, precepts, word, judgments). Before you read, ask the Lord to reveal His character and heart to you. Ponder who He is and how He loves you.

Back to Proverbs 3. Notice that the first verse says *"do not forget my law."* But then it says, *"let your **heart** keep my commands."* What is this? This leads me to believe that keeping God's commands is a heart issue. God doesn't just want us to simply store them in our noodles so we can calculate what we get. He wants these commands and promises to be in our heart, the very center of our being, the center of our thoughts, our feelings, our emotions, our desires. David meditated on His words *"day and night."* David was a man after God's own heart. He knew God intimately—he became acquainted with God's own heart.

God's commands promised a long life, protection, honor, vitality, direction, esteem, and also peace with others, yes. But, meditating on God's commands promised long life and *peace* and intimacy with his Creator God.

Can we make His law a part of us so we can say, like David, "Oh how I LOVE YOUR INSTRUCTIONS. I think about them all day long" and then draw close to God's heart?

PROMISES TO MEMORIZE

The law of the Lord is perfect, converting the soul; the testimony of the Lord is sure, making wise the simple; the statutes of the Lord are right, rejoicing the heart; the commandment of the Lord is pure, enlightening the eyes; the fear of the Lord is clean, enduring forever; the judgments of the Lord are true and righteous altogether (Psalm 19:7-9 NKJV)

Jesus said to him, "You shall love the Lord your God with all your heart, with all your soul, and with all your mind." This is the first and great commandment. And the second is like it: "You shall love your neighbor as yourself." On these two commandments hang all the Law and the Prophets (Matthew 22:37-40 NKJV).

All the paths of the Lord are mercy and truth. To such as keep His covenant and His testimonies (Psalm 25:10 NKJV).

Blessed is the man who walks not in the counsel of the ungodly, nor stands in the path of sinners, nor sits in the seat of the scornful; but his delight is in the law of the Lord, and in His law he meditates day and night (Psalm 1:1-2 NKJV).

Prayer

Lord, help me to meditate on Your word so that I can understand Your heart and know Your promises and experience Your peace. Thank You, Lord, for Your commands.

What promise has God given you today?

JAIMEE FELBER

I have two favorite scriptures that I have held onto very tightly over the past years. One of them is Romans 8:25-27 which says:

But if we hope for what we do not yet see, we wait for it patiently. In the same way, the Spirit helps us in our weakness. For we do not know how we ought to pray, but the Spirit Himself intercedes for us with groans too deep for words. And He who searches our hearts knows the mind of the Spirit, because the Spirit intercedes for the saints according to the will of God.

I love this verse when I have gone through things where I don't even know what to pray for or don't know how to pray because I just don't even know what I want or what would be best—and this verse is reassurance that I do not have to have the answers and do not have to know exactly what to pray for. The Holy Spirit will take care of it.

And another favorite is Matthew 6:26-27, which is of course:

Look at the birds of the air; they do not sow or reap or store away in barns and yet your heavenly Father feeds them. Are you not much more valuable than they? Who of you by worrying can add a single hour to this life?

That's my favorite to look to when I catch myself worrying.

MANDY YAMAMOTO

"For I know the plans I have for you," declares the Lord, "plans to prosper you and not to harm you, plans to give you hope and a future" (Jeremiah 29:11 NIV).

When we don't see immediate results, we can be faithful because of the ultimate blessings and benefits: things happen for a reason; there's a blessing in everything.

God won't give you what you cannot handle, but surely you will be tested first to see if you can be trusted by Him.

These are promises that get me through the thick and thin times to help me remain optimistic throughout.

Chapter 9

HE COMES TO US AND CARES FOR US

I will not leave you as orphans; I will come to you.
—JOHN 14:18 NIV

Have you ever felt abandoned? Like you're on an island or in the desert all alone? I'm sure we all go through times like these. We feel like the wind has been knocked out of us. We find ourselves unable to think or even feel. We ask, "Lord, are You there? Have You forgotten me? Are You listening?" Yes, I asked these questions when Paul and I moved (from where I thought I would live until my time to go to Heaven) to North Carolina. Our daughter had gotten married and moved to Colorado. Paul Edward and Melanie were getting married a few months after Mark and Gretchen. We were moving our youngest son,

Thom, away from his life-long friends. Our friends, who we had laughed with, cried with, went to church with and our children had grown up with for 13 years, were nowhere to be found. My heart was broken, and I didn't know what God was up to.

We settled into our life in North Carolina and started Bible School. Before we graduated, we had an invitation from a pastor from Indian Trail, NC, to come preach and sing on Sunday. We hadn't met this pastor, but a friend had recommended he have us minister one Sunday.

Mike Whitson, the pastor of Indian Trail Baptist Church, was told about Paul's past adultery, and since he'd never met us, he decided to cancel the meeting. So, he asked us to meet him at the local restaurant where he was planning on letting us know he couldn't have us at his church. Paul and I waited for two hours, but Mike didn't show up. When we got home, there was a message on our phone from him, "My transmission in my brand-new, maintenance-free car went out on me while driving up the mountain. Can we meet next week?" So, we made plans for the following week. This happened three times. First the transmission, then the engine, then another transmission. All brand-new, maintenance-free vehicles. After the third break-down, Mike said, "Okay, God, what are You trying to tell me?" Mike's own words: "If you don't help restore this man and his wife, I will remove my protecting hand from you and let you fall in the same sin" (Galatians 6:1). Mike decided to have us at his church.

We had a glorious Sunday, and Mike invited us back for a week-long meeting. A woman from his church gave us a car during this meeting. It was an '80s Pontiac Parisian Station Wagon that needed some work. We were grateful for her generosity, but we didn't need a car. So, we asked Mike if they would mind if we sold it. We put an ad in the paper in Asheville, North Carolina. We described the condition of the car and the price, and we waited.

One evening we got a call from a young man named Mike Lochner. He said he wanted to buy the car. When Paul asked him how he heard about the car, he said he was driving through Asheville and saw the ad in the paper. Paul asked him where he was from. He said, "Madison, Wisconsin." We thought it was a joke being played on us. Madison would be approximately 1,000 miles from North Carolina. Why would anyone drive 1,000 miles to buy a run-down Pontiac? Paul told him to make sure he wanted the car, and if he did, call back tomorrow. Surely, he wouldn't call back! We shared this with our Bible school friends and we all had a good laugh. The following night, Mike called back. Paul was surprised, "Mike, I know there are cars for sale between here and Madison that you can buy." But Mike said he knew this car was the one he was supposed to have. Really? He told us he would be coming in on the bus that week to get the car. We were shaking our heads wondering if we should even go to the bus station. This can't be right!

Paul and I headed to the bus station on Tunnel Road in Asheville still wondering if this was a joke. There's only one way in and one way out of the station. There wasn't a bus or a vehicle around. Paul walked into the station and asked the manager if the bus from Madison was due. He was told that there wasn't even a bus due in that day. There was only the station attendant in the building. As Paul was walking back to the van, a man came around the corner from the station and called his name. Paul turned around and there was Mike. He was stooped over in pain. He said he had been riding on the bus for 24 hours. We couldn't believe our eyes.

Mike got in the van and Paul started to back out of the bus station, but curious, he stopped the van. "Mike" he asked, "What are you doing here?" Mike's answer was, "I don't know. But all the way here I have been reading the confessions of St. Augustine asking God to show me what's truth." So, we looked at each other believing that God had sent him so we could share the gospel with him. We told him we would take him to check out the car, but he said it wasn't necessary. He was sure it was okay, but Paul made him look at it anyway. He explained the things that needed to be fixed. Mike gave Paul a cashier's check, so we went by the bank and deposited it...just in case! We then took him to our apartment and shared the gospel. He called his wife, Ruth, and told her he had gotten saved. Ruth told Paul that she had been praying for Mike to be saved.

We loaded Mike up with cassettes and books. As he drove out of the complex, he went the wrong way. We were wondering if he could find his way back to Madison since he couldn't even find his way out of the complex.

The reason I'm sharing this story, which still amazes Paul and me today, is that God spoke to my heart as Mike was driving away and said, "My dear child, I haven't forgotten you. I know right where you live." Yes, dear friend, God said He would never leave us or forsake us. He will never abandon us.

We tried to get in touch with Mike after he left, but there was no Mike Lochner to be found. We called the number he used to call his wife, but there was no such number. So, where did Mike come from? We believe God sent an angel to encourage us on our journey, to remind us that He never leaves us or forsakes us (Hebrews 13:2). I read a statement the other day that said, "If God wants me, He knows where to find me." As the promise in John 14 says, *"I will come to you."*

PROMISES TO MEMORIZE AND MEDITATE UPON

Keep your life free from love of money, and be content with what you have, for he has said, "I will never leave you nor forsake you" (Hebrews 13:5)

Teaching them to observe all that I have commanded you. And behold, I am with you always, to the end of the age (Matthew 28:20).

Have I not commanded you? Be strong and courageous. Do not be frightened, and do not be dismayed, for the Lord your God is with you wherever you go (Joshua 1:9).

Where shall I go from your Spirit? Or where shall I flee from your presence? If I ascend to heaven, you are there! If I make my bed in Sheol, you are there! If I take the wings of the morning and dwell in the uttermost parts of the sea, even there your hand shall lead me, and your right hand shall hold me. If I say, surely the darkness shall cover me even the night shall be light about me. Yea, the darkness hideth not from thee; but the night shineth as the day: the darkness and the light are both alike to thee (Psalm 139: 7-12).

Prayer

Father, thank You for Your loving care, which is continual. You never give up on me. You patiently work in my heart. No matter where I am, You are with me. "Lord, you have granted me life and steadfast love, and your care has preserved my spirit" (Job 10:12). Amen.

What promise has God given to you today?

SANDY YUEN

I know how to be abased, and I know how to abound. Everywhere and in all things I have learned both to be full and to be hungry, both to abound and to suffer need (Philippians 4:12).

This is the verse that spoke to me since I had lived growing up with little, and then to live with plenty. I realized God has been with me and protecting me and watching over me to get me to VANCOUVER to meet Dan who was in the Amway business already! For me, I didn't feel any different, with little or plenty! I just knew God had provided my every need at every stage of my life. I have been blessed to be used by God to serve.

NORMA FOGLIO

There hath no temptation taken you but such as is common to man: but God is faithful, who will not suffer you to be tempted above that ye are able; but will with the temptation also make a way to escape, that ye may be able to bear it (1 Corinthians 10:13).

I keep thinking, when you can't even pray for yourself or your situation, that your friends are lifting you up in prayer. I survive on that. I don't even have an abundance of grace, other than the grace God abundantly gives. God sees me much stronger than I see myself. I keep thinking, I know the Lord won't give me more than I can handle. I don't know if I prayed that... I just keep seeing that verse and saying I must believe this.

LEXIE BAKER

Two promises from God's word:

Yet who knows if you have come to the kingdom for a such a time as this? (Esther 4:14).

Years ago, at the beginning of my business journey, I felt the Lord speaking this to my heart. It has been an incredible reminder when it would be so easy to let up, give in, or be discouraged that God has brought us to things and times in this world for a purpose. His will and plan will be accomplished. I now have to decide to be obedient and trust that He has the strength and power to complete His plan even if I don't feel like I can do it.

He who dwells in the secret place of the Most High Shall abide under the shadow of the Almighty. I will say of the LORD, "He is my refuge and my fortress; My God, in Him I will trust." Surely He shall deliver you from the snare of the fowler And from the perilous pestilence. He shall cover you with His feathers, And under His wings you shall take refuge; His truth shall be your shield and buckler. You shall not be afraid of the terror by night, nor of the arrow that flies by day, nor of the pestilence that walks in darkness, nor of the destruction that lays waste at noonday. A thousand may fall at your side, and ten thousand at your right hand; but it shall not come near you. Only with your eyes shall you look, and see the reward of the wicked. Because you have made the LORD, who is my refuge, even the Most High, your dwelling place, no evil shall befall you, nor shall any plague come near your dwelling; for He shall give His angels charge over you, to keep you in all your ways. In their hands they shall bear you up, lest you dash your foot against a stone. You shall tread upon the lion and the cobra, the young lion and the serpent you shall trample underfoot. "Because he has set his love upon Me, therefore I will deliver him; I will set him on high, because he has known My name. He shall call upon Me, and I will answer him; I will be with him in trouble; I will deliver him and honor him. With long life I will satisfy him And show him My salvation" (Psalm 91:1-16 NKJV).

When difficult things happened in my life: my brother overdosing on my living room floor, being in the hospital with unknown cause bleeding, our son Rogan's lack of movement 5 days before his due date while I was pregnant and not knowing what was happening—to name a few times. Reading and praying Psalm 91 is a large part of how I made it through and trusted that no matter what, our Lord can be trusted.

Chapter 10

JUDGES OR VESSELS OF HONOR

Do not judge and criticize and condemn [others unfairly with an attitude of self-righteous superiority as though assuming the office of a judge], so that you will not be judged [unfairly]. For just as you [hypocritically] judge others [when you are sinful and unrepentant], so will you be judged; and in accordance with your standard of measure [used to pass out judgment], judgment will be measured to you.

—MATTHEW 7:1-2 AMP

This passage of scripture seems to be in the negative. Don't judge, criticize, or condemn, because when you do, you get it returned to you. In other words, God uses the same measuring stick as you do with others. This is a great truth that we all desperately need, daily. We can all be judgmental and critical. Now, we may lie to ourselves and say we're just "sizing" up the person or situation, but God calls our sizing-up, sin!

We must remember: we're not the judge! Our neighbors don't have to give an account to us, and we don't have to give an account to anyone, but to God. In Romans 14, we read that every knee will bow, and everyone will confess Christ as Lord, and we are accountable to God, not man.

I don't know about you, but I can jump to conclusions many times or make snap judgments about someone. I try to keep in mind that I don't have all the facts or really know what's going on in a person's life, so I can't really judge them according to my impressions.

How do we judge others? We assume things about a person at first glance. We don't know them, but because of the way they look we assume the worst, or maybe the best. Or, we may have heard others say things about them, so we judge according to the biases of others. Or, we may judge them because of our insecurities because we compare ourselves to them.

In First Samuel, we read the story of Saul. He was evidently a very tall man and probably very handsome. The people of Israel wanted a king. They didn't care what God thought. They wanted who and what they wanted. God said He had rejected Saul, and, yet, because of his appearance, they chose him to be king. God says that man looks on the outward, but He looks at our heart.

Ephesians 4:29 tells us to speak only what will minister grace to the one we are speaking to. Watch the way you talk!

Speak words that heal and encourage! Stop judging others! I'm speaking to myself as I write this!

I remember a story an evangelist friend shared during a sermon years ago. He was preaching at a church when a woman walked in with her hair pulled to the side of her face across one eye. She was a beautiful woman, and this made her look very sexy. His judgment of her was that of a loose woman or one trying to be like Hollywood, so he hit on that subject during his message: how sinful it was to call attention to oneself. After a couple of nights of meetings, the woman was leaving the church and went by to shake the evangelist's hand to let him know how much she had enjoyed the messages. As she moved her head, the evangelist saw that under her hair was a very distorted face. She had been burned as a child, so she was trying to cover up her scars. Was he grieved at his assumption? Absolutely! He had judged her without knowing all the facts. We can be God's agent to affirm and help heal these scars or we can add to them. It was a defining moment in light of her generous spirit toward him.

I must remind myself, and I have often told my children and grandchildren, that we shouldn't judge a young person by what we see or hear. We have no idea what God is doing or will do in their lives. If people went back and judged Paul and me in our early years, and I'm sure some have, they would have given us NO hope. However, God never gave up on us. He was, and still is, sanctifying us. He doesn't leave us as we are. He's the Potter. We are the clay. He is molding and making us—and you—His vessels of honor!

PROMISES TO MEMORIZE OR MEDITATE UPON

Therefore you have no excuse, O man, every one of you who judges. For in passing judgment on another you condemn yourself, because you, the judge, practice the very same things. We know that the judgment of God rightly falls on those who practice such things. Do you suppose, O man—you who judge those who practice such things and yet do them yourself—that you will escape the judgment of God? (Romans 2:1-3 ESV).

To speak evil of no one, to avoid quarreling, to be gentle, and to show perfect courtesy toward all people. For we ourselves were once foolish, disobedient, led astray, slaves to various passions and pleasures, passing our days in malice and envy, hated by others and hating one another. But when the goodness and loving kindness of God our Savior appeared, he saved us, not because of works done by us in righteousness, but according to his own mercy, by the washing of regeneration and renewal of the Holy Spirit, whom he poured out on us richly through Jesus Christ our Savior (Titus 2:3-7 ESV).

But the Lord said to Samuel, "Do not look on his appearance or on the height of his stature, because I have rejected him. For the Lord sees not as man sees; man looks on the outward appearance, but the Lord looks on the heart" (1 Samuel 16:7 ESV).

Prayer

Lord, You know how judgmental I can get. I ask forgiveness, You, alone, are the one who judges a person's ways and feelings. Help me to keep my thoughts to myself and let You take care of every situation where I would be judgmental "Let no corrupting talk come out of your mouths, but only such as is good for building up, as fits the occasion, that it may give grace to those who hear" (Ephesians 4:29. ESV). Amen.

What promise has He given you today?

PAM KIZIRIAN

Be strong and of a good courage, fear not, nor be afraid of them: for the Lord thy God, he it is that doth go with thee; he will not fail thee, nor forsake thee. And Moses called unto Joshua and said unto him in the sight of all Israel, Be strong and of a good courage: for thou must go with this people unto the land which the Lord hath sworn unto their fathers to give them; and thou shalt cause them to inherit it (Deuteronomy 31:6-7 KJV).

JUDY HEAD

By faith even Sarah herself received power to conceive seed when she was past age, since she counted him faithful who had promised (Hebrews 11:11).

Years ago, as I began to meditate on this scripture it seemed to come alive. Every time I thought on it the Lord would take me into a new revelation of its truths for me today in my life. The seed is the Word of God: His promises. Sarah had been barren all her life even though she desired with all her heart to conceive. Her physical body could not receive the seed. And in her culture, a barren woman was looked on as cursed of God, and now she is too old, according to the natural way of life. Her womb is dead. But, there came a moment in time, God's time, when Sarah's faith and God's faithfulness became one, and Sarah conceived God's promise: Her physical body, healed. Her image of being cursed changed to Blessed of God. Her dead womb, His Word, was conceived and became manifest in the physical realm. I, like Sarah, desired with all my heart to have God's promises come alive in my life and my family's lives. I, like Sarah, looked at the blessings in Deuteronomy and wondered, questioned, and grieved. Why? And I, like Sarah, heard the enemies lies, "You have never been able to conceive God's promise. Stop believing! Focus on your past failure. Focus on your disappointments! It will be easier and less stressful to just give up and accept life as it is."

There is a scene in the movie, *The Miracle Worker*, based on the life of Helen Keller and her teacher, Anne Sullivan. Anne was almost blind, and Helen was deaf and blind. Helen groped through life in darkness and silence unable to understand the world around her. Anne was trying to teach her sign language, but it was nothing more to her than a parrot repeating words. But then one day, a moment in time, God's time, with teacher holding her hand under running water, they connected. Helen was everywhere in her excitement, dragging her teacher with her asking, "What is this?" That is a picture of me the moment my teacher, the Holy Spirit, immersed me in the living Water of God's Word, His promises. His living Word pierced into my darkness and manifested the Promise in the Language of Heaven.

Chapter 11

NEEDY? OBTAIN MERCY AND FIND GRACE

Let us therefore come boldly unto the throne of grace, that we may obtain mercy, and find grace to help in time of need.

—Hebrews 4:16 KJV

I can't tell you how many times I've prayed this prayer, "Lord, You said I could come boldly to your throne of grace. I need help!" I'm sure you have prayed this many times, also. What a privilege to come into His throne room knowing that the Creator of the universe beckons us to come. We now have access to our heavenly Father because of Christ.

In John chapter 8, there's a wonderful picture of mercy and grace. Jesus was surrounded by swarms of people while teaching in the temple, and guess who shows up?

The religion scholars and Pharisees led in a woman who had been caught in an act of adultery. They stood her in plain sight of everyone and said, "Teacher, this woman was caught red-handed in the act of adultery. Moses, in the Law, gives orders to stone such persons. What do you say?" They were trying to trap him into saying something incriminating so they could bring charges against him. Jesus, bent down and wrote with his finger in the dirt. They kept at him, badgering him. He straightened up and said, "The sinless one among you, go first: Throw the stone." Bending down again, he wrote some more in the dirt. Hearing that, they walked away, one after another, beginning with the oldest. The woman was left alone. Jesus stood up and spoke to her. "Woman, where are they? Does no one condemn you?" "No one, Master." "Neither do I," said Jesus. "Go on your way. From now on, don't sin" (John 8:1-11 The Message).

Can you imagine the shame and fear of this woman? Even if she had a bedsheet carelessly strewn about her, her sin was fully exposed—guilty! She was guilty! It was a cruel time and the crowd watching was thirsty for her retribution. Most were ready with stone clasped in hand. The Pharisees were indignant—tired of this Jesus crossing what they knew to be true. They were the experts. Now, not only did they catch a sinner, they trapped this crazy, righteous charlatan! Imagine claiming He was a teacher of the law and then crossing the law. But, this time, they had Him dead to rights! Haha! They caught her in the act—guilty! Jesus was trapped! It was a two birds with one stone day! They were smug exchanging sidelong glances with one another. The air was thick with suspense. Surely she would be stoned and He would be led off to face His demise. Now Jesus, calm—thoughtful, stoops down and scratches the sand with a twig. If there were pins that day, you would hear them drop. The quiet is good—His words are measured and resonate in the stillness...

"The sinless one among you, go first" (John 8:7).

What? The sinless one go first? Who could profess to be sinless? Slowly, at first, then one after the other come the sound of rocks hitting the dusty, dry ground. And the ones with the heaviest stones begin leaving first.

Oh that those words would fill our thoughts when we have a judgmental stone posed in our hand and ready to throw—Let the sinless among you go first.

Who can really describe God's grace and mercy? The definition that is given for grace is God's free and unmerited favor not only in salvation but in our daily lives. There's nothing we did to merit it. There's nothing we can do to earn it. It's a free gift given to us by our loving heavenly Father. I believe grace and mercy go hand in hand. Can there be one without the other?

When God in Jesus took the punishment for our sins upon himself, he didn't give us what we deserve (eternal condemnation and separation from him). What incredible mercy! But God didn't stop there.

He continually gives us what we don't deserve—
the next beat of our hearts, the air in our lungs, the
food we eat, the clothes on our back, the privilege of
living on his earth, our different friends and family
members, experiencing the beauty of his creation,
etc. Plus, he gave us the precious, invaluable gift of
eternal life—an eternal relationship with his Son,
Jesus—something we don't deserve. What amazing
grace![1]

I was reading one of my devotionals when I came across
this prayer.

I have no resume to hold before You, no track record
of accomplishments, no letters of commendation,
no rights of birth or ethnicity. I hold nothing that
would place You in my debt; nothing that could
curry Your favor, nothing that would obligate
You. I wish unbridled zeal would commend me to
You. I wish unbroken obedience would draw Your
attention. I wish model wisdom and model love
would convince You that I'm worthy. But I have
none of these things to offer You. I stand before
you with shoulders bent and hands that are empty.
I approach You with no argument in my mind or
words to offer in my defense. I stand before you
naked and undeserving, broken and weak. I am
quite aware of the duplicity of my heart, the evil
of my choices, and the failure of my behavior, but I
am not afraid because I stand before You with one

argument. This argument is enough. This plea is sufficient. This argument the only thing that could ever give me courage, rest, and sturdy hope. So, I come before You with this plea, Your mercy.[2]

In the Old Testament, the curtain (veil) that was set up in the Tabernacle was a division that kept all out except the High Priest. He, alone, was allowed into the Holy of Holies. The High Priest had to enter the tabernacle through the curtain which separated the people from the Holy of Holies, and he would make a sacrifice every year for the sins of the people. But Hebrews 10 tells us that the blood of bulls and goats could never take away sins. The blood might cover the sins, but it could not wash them away. When Christ died, and shed His blood, He paid the ultimate price for the sins of the world, once and for all (1 Timothy 2:5). Christ is our Mediator. The curtain that separated us from entering the Holy of Holies was torn in two the moment Christ died on the cross. This opened the way for us ALL to enter God's throne room. He is our ultimate High Priest. We enter God's presence through His shed blood (Matthew 27) which is sprinkled on the Mercy seat. It is through Mercy that God relates to man and man relates to God.

Lamentations 3:22-23 assures us that God's *steadfast* love never ceases and His mercies *never* end. His promise is that His mercies are new *every* morning. Great is His faithfulness. Remember, He is faithful! We may not be faithful or believe at times, but He is always faithful (2 Timothy 2:13). He loves us on our good days and our bad days. His gift of grace and mercy and love is ours forever.

God's mercy is my rest and my hope. It makes me bold. Mercy lets me know that God is here and that He hears me. His mercy tells me how to act. It compels me to forgive, restore and strengthen. Mercy triumphs over judgment (James 2:13), and You, O Lord, are mercy!

Promises to Memorize or Meditate Upon

All the paths of the LORD are steadfast love and faithfulness, for those who keep his covenant and his testimonies (Psalm 25:10 ESV).

Therefore, in all things He had to be made like His brethren, that He might be a merciful and faithful High Priest in things pertaining to God, to make propitiation for the sins of the people. For in that He Himself has suffered, being tempted, He is able to aid those who are tempted (Hebrews 2:17-18 NKJV).

Seeing then that we have a great High Priest who has passed through the heavens, Jesus the Son of God, let us hold fast our confession. For we do not have a High Priest who cannot sympathize with our weaknesses, but was in all points tempted as we are, yet without sin. Let us therefore come boldly to the throne of grace, that we may obtain mercy and find grace to help in time of need (Hebrews 4:14-16 NKJV).

When I thought, "My foot slips," your steadfast love, O LORD, held me up. When the cares of my heart are many, your consolations cheer my soul (Psalm 94:18-19 ESV).

With the merciful you will show Yourself merciful... (2 Samuel 22:26 NKJV).

But you, O Lord, are a God merciful and gracious, slow to anger and abounding in steadfast love and faithfulness (Psalm 86:15 ESV).

Prayer

Father, I am so grateful for the privilege to come before Your throne boldly and seek Your face. Thank You for the help we find; for Your grace and mercy every time we are in need. Thank You for the grace to have hope, rest and peace. You restore and strengthen me, daily through Your Word. I am blessed. Amen.

What promise has God given you today?

SANDY SEARS

Yet this I call to mind and therefore I have hope: Because of the Lord's great love we are not consumed, for his compassions never fail. They are new every morning; great is your faithfulness (Lamentations 3:21-23 NIV).

Here is the promise that is important to me right now in my life. I am just so grateful for the Lord's forgiveness! For I do deserve to be "consumed." But because of His great compassion and faithfulness because He willingly went to the cross, I am forgiven. I am continually seeking forgiveness for my sins and holding onto the hope that someday sin will be no more. What a glorious day that will be!

When I got this promise from Sandy, I was reading the same verses in Lamentations. Evidently, I need to be reminded of this promise again and again. What is amazing about God's Word is that it is alive. We can read a passage of scripture over and over and receive something new each time. God ministers to us exactly what we need, when we need it. Great is His faithfulness. It can never be said enough.

LESLIE HALL

The fear of the LORD tendeth to life: and he that hath it shall abide satisfied; he shall not be visited with evil (Proverbs 19:23 KJV).

When you live a life of abandoned love, surrendered before the awe of God, here's what *you'll experience:* Abundant life. Continual protection. And complete satisfaction!

When I am walking close to God, I can trust that His plans for me are good. He has already written my whole story and He has assignments for me. He gifted me with strengths that it are up to me to discover. When I am walking in my strengths, I am able to flow easily to be a light that helps dispel the darkness.

Yes, like Leslie said, we are the light of the world. We should let our light shine brightly before everyone. When we do, they will see our good works and our heavenly Father will get the glory (Matthew 5).

GEORGIA LEE PURYEAR

This is the day that the Lord has made, we will rejoice and be glad in it (Psalm 118:24).

For me, this is the promise of Jesus that I have held onto and hold onto every day. Through the sadness and the tears and through the joy and the laughter in my life. I know that He is sovereign over it all. I am forever grateful.

JOYA BAKER

I have used promises in my life since I was a child that my parents passed down to me, but this one I use often when traveling. I don't like to fly. I hate turbulence—so there was one time when I was flying from Walla Walla, Washington, to Seattle and the pilot came on the intercom on the little plane and said, "This is going to be a roller coaster flight, so if you have any Dramamine, I'd recommend you take it." I saw the flight attendant outside the plane throwing up and I began to pray right then, and I prayed out loud.

So, I begin to pray like I do on all my flights, and I bind satan—"In the name of Jesus Christ I bind you satan and all your angels from the airways from this flight from this plane, from these wings, from the passenger to the pilots in the name of Jesus Christ I bind you satan from this flight. Please let this flight be smooth and set us gently down in Seattle."

Well, we left Walla Walla and landed in Seattle and the pilot came on as we were landing and said, "Well, I don't know how to explain it but that was the smoothest flight. We had zero turbulence." When we walked off the plane, and that's one of those tiny planes, I told him I know why we didn't have turbulence: "I prayed and I bound satan in the name of Jesus Christ, and God got us here safely." He smiled and I got off the plane. I've used that many, many times. I do it often and God answers my prayers and is true to His promise.

ENDNOTES

1. David Chadwick, *From Superficial to Significant,* (Eugene, OR: Harvest House, 2001), 86.

2. Paul David Tripp, *A Shelter in the Time of Storm: Meditations on God and Trouble* (Wheaton, IL: Crossway Books, 2009), 60.

Chapter 12

SPEAKING LIFE OR DEATH

Death and life are in the power of the tongue, and those who love it and indulge it will eat its fruit and bear the consequences of their words.
            —PROVERBS 18:21 AMP

Words kill, words give life; they're either poison or fruit—you choose.
            —PROVERBS 18:21 THE MESSAGE

During WWII a doctor with the British army in North Africa made his rounds of patients who were all lying on stretchers. Every morning he greeted each patient with the same two sentences: How are you? And show me your tongue. The first question was how are you, but he didn't wait for the answer. He immediately said, show me your tongue. When the patient stuck out his tongue, the doctor looked carefully at it. Then he would form the estimate of the patient's condition from the look of his tongue rather than how the patient answered the question, "How are you?"[1]

I believe, along with the man telling this story, that God does the same with us as the doctor did with his patients. God may ask, how are you? And we may give an estimate of our condition. But, if God asks us to show Him our tongue, what would He see? The state of our tongues is a very sure guide to our spiritual condition, as we read from the scripture.

We may deceive ourselves about the state of our hearts with all sorts of ideas about our own goodness, purity or righteousness, but the sure and unfailing indicator is what comes out of our mouths.

> *Even so every good tree bringeth forth good fruit; but a corrupt tree bringeth forth evil fruit. A good tree cannot bring forth evil fruit, neither can a corrupt tree bring forth good fruit. Every tree that bringeth not forth good fruit is hewn down and cast into the fire. Wherefore by their fruits ye shall know them* (Matthew 7:17-20 KJV).

James deals in depth with this issue in our lives. *"If anyone among you thinks he is religious, and does not bridle his tongue but deceives his own heart, this one's religion is useless"* (James 1:26). It doesn't matter how religious we may claim to be. We may attend church, sing hymns or praise songs, and do other things that are expected of religious people. These things are good, and we may do all of these, but if we do not keep our tongues under control, our religion is worthless and unacceptable to God. May God grant that we all face up to this issue. The first chapter of James is strong about the control of our tongue and the first two chapters of Proverbs are almost completely about the use of our words and our tongue. We need to read this wisdom, meditate and pray on it, digest it.

James 3 talks about bits in the mouths of horses (physical strength); a rudder that steers ships (strong winds and waves, and powerful forces yet a small rudder can change the whole course of a ship); the tongue is a fire (Only you can prevent forest fires). Proverbs 26:20 says, *"Where there is no wood, the fire goes out...."* The Message translation says: *"When you run out of wood, the fire goes out; when the gossip ends, the quarrel dies down."*

We should ask ourselves how to deal with our heart/tongue issues. When we don't deal with our problem based on truth, it is sin! Holy Spirit is the Spirit of truth. We must confess and receive forgiveness. We must yield to God's Holy Spirit and refuse to sin. His Holy Spirit is the only Person in the universe who can give us the power to control our tongues. Adrian Rogers, a Christian pastor, said, "The sign that you are Spirit-filled is not the ability to speak in a language (tongue) you have never learned, but the ability to control the one tongue we do have."[2]

Paul and I had to deal with our tongue issues (still do from time to time) when God brought us to devastation in the 1980s. We continually indulged our tongue and we most certainly did reap the consequences. Oh, it wasn't immediately, but in time,

God brought us to repentance. We were so critical of people and gossiped about everyone and anything. Believe me, you don't want God to bring you to this place. You can repent of your sin against God and His children without Him having to deal with you. But you must recognize it as sin, confess, and receive forgiveness. Repent means to turn. You must turn from your sinful ways and refuse to gossip or malign anyone's character. It doesn't matter if you know what you're saying is true or not. It's still doing damage to the person you are speaking about, and yourself.

In my own life, it has helped me to fend off speaking about others by following two guidelines. These have helped me immensely. The first is that I will only speak directly to the person in question or the person I "feel" at odds with or is talking about me. Notice I said "feel" at odds with. There is always more than a chance that I have the wrong impression right from the beginning, or I have heard a wrong report or even if the report is accurate it is none of my business unless it has to do with me. So, I have to start at the beginning recognizing that I could be wrong and any information that has filtered through to me could be tainted. So, I will not go from person to person clarifying second-hand information. No, I am steadfast in my resolve to only go to the person I feel may be at odds with me. Mum's the word to anyone else. I am resolved to go to the person who was talking and that person only.

The second guideline is as important as the first. That is I do not accuse! I ask questions with the intent that whatever obstacle or judgment lies between me and the person I am talking to (in private) will be rectified and the relationship restored. The goal is to not prove that I am right or the other person is wrong, but that any tear in a relationship is mended. When that is mended, almost any other problem can be resolved and forgiveness can be extended. It is okay then to say, "I'm sorry, I was feeling hurt because I was told that in some form or fashion you were making fun of me or belittling me (or simply talking about me). It hurts me to have people talking about my private matters. Please don't talk about me—I'd just rather you talk with me if you have to talk at all."

So, don't talk to others about the person in question. Talk to the person in question directly if you have any business in it. Secondly, ask questions, restore relationships, and kindly request they don't talk to others. We can be kind and merciful but let them know sadly, that it feels embarrassing and hurtful. Well, doesn't it?

Do you remember when you were young, and you wanted your siblings to not tell on you? I know I would call my sisters blabbermouth! Tattletale! Bigmouth! These are a few of the words used for gossipers. I don't know about you, but I don't want to be known as a gossiper, blabbermouth, tattletale, or bigmouth. If someone gossips to you, they will gossip about you!

We used to play the Whisper Game. You whisper something in someone's ear and they whisper to the next person, and so on. By the time you get to the end of the circle, it's amazing what the last person heard. It was nothing like what the first person said. This is how gossip goes. Everyone lends their own thoughts to what was originally said. DON'T BE

A GOSSIPER! As Thumper's (Bambi) mother said, "If you can't say anything good, don't say anything at all."[3] You will save yourself a lot of heartache. Words spoken in a whisper are often heard in the most surprising places.

PROMISES TO MEMORIZE

Whoever desires to love life and see good days, let him keep his tongue from evil and his lips from speaking deceit (1 Peter 3:10 ESV).

When words are many, transgression is not lacking, but whoever restrains his lips is prudent (Proverbs 10:19 ESV).

...Hear and understand: it is not what goes into the mouth that defiles a person, but what comes out of the mouth; this defiles a person (Matthew 15:10 NASB).

Whoever keeps his mouth and his tongue keeps himself out of trouble (Proverbs 21:23 ESV).

Whoever restrains his words has knowledge, and he who has a cool spirit is a man of understanding. Even a fool who keeps silent is considered wise; when he closes his lips, he is deemed intelligent (Proverbs 17:27 ESV).

Let no corrupt communication proceed out of your mouth, but that which is good to the use of edifying, that it may minister grace unto the hearers (Ephesians 4:29 NKJV).

Prayer

Lord, truly my tongue needs to continually be tamed by Your Holy Spirit. I don't want words that are critical or any corrupt communication to come out of my mouth. I want to use my tongue to edify, to encourage and uplift. "Set a watch, O LORD, before my mouth; keep the door of my lips" (Psalm 141:3 KJV). Amen.

What promise has God given to you today?

CHRIS HARIMOTO

God is our refuge and strength, a helper who is always found in times of trouble (Psalm 46:1 NKJV).

A refuge is a safe place, a trusted place or person. It is something or someone you can run to that will take care of you and make you feel safe and secure. When we choose to take refuge in God, we are giving that trust to Him—choosing to believe He is our safe place, our strength and helper. We trust His promises and His ways. So often we trust and rely on ourselves more than we do God. Too often we respond to our carnal feelings instead of having faith in God, whom we cannot necessarily touch, taste, hear, smell, or see.

MARCIE WHALEN

Do not fear, for I am with you; Do not anxiously look about you, for I am your God; I will strengthen you, surely I will help you, Surely I will uphold you with My righteous right hand (Isaiah 41:10 NASB 1995).

I love this verse and this translation in particular because it is so reassuring and starts off by addressing two of the emotions I am most likely to fall into: fear and anxiety. But God promises me—there is nothing to fear! For He is with me. And I need not be anxious when He is my God who will strengthen me and help me and uphold me! This promise is extra reassuring with the use of the word "surely"—used to emphasize the firm belief that what is being said is true and to assure and give confidence to the reader. This is one of the most powerful promises I can cling to. I am comforted and awed when I read it.

VALERIE GONZER

And we know that for those who love God all things work together for good, for those who are called according to his purpose (Romans 8:28 ESV).

I love piano music and one of my favorite songs is, "Surely the Presence of the Lord is in This Place." This song and verse remind me of God's faithfulness to Tom and me through our 50 years of marriage. Through the fear, finances, children, work, and just daily life, God has been faithful. He has used every dumb thing we've done into something good, like He promised. We know that not all things are good in themselves, but God uses everything for our good and His glory.

ENDNOTES

1. Derek Prince, *On Experiencing God's Power* (New Kensington, PA: Whitaker House, 1998), 6.

2. Adrian Rodgers quote is taken from a sermon entitled: You Are a Gifted Child (1 Cor.12:1-12); https://www.lwf.org/pdfs/2201-YOU-ARE-A-GIFTED-CHILD.docx; accessed November 9, 2021.

3. Quote from Gene Edwards, *The Triumph*.(Jacksonville, FL: SeedSowers Pub., 1995), 4.

Chapter 13

OUT OF THE DEPTHS, HE HEARS

Out of the depths I cry to you, O LORD! O Lord,
hear my voice! Let your ears be attentive to the voice
of my pleas for mercy! If you, O LORD, should mark
iniquities, O Lord, who could stand? But with you
there is forgiveness, that you may be feared. I wait for
the LORD, my soul waits, and in his word I hope;
my soul waits for the Lord more than watchmen for
the morning, more than watchmen for the morning.
— PSALM 130:1-6 ESV

What are these depths the psalmist speaks of? Out of the depths of his soul the psalmist waits for the Lord. There he pleads for mercy. This deep place is a place of anguish, need, and longing that cannot be framed in words. It is a place that can only be touched and understood by the Lord. In Psalm 42:7, the psalmist uses the metaphor of the sea—deep waters, deep churning waters: *"Deep calls unto deep…Your waves and billows have gone over me"* says the psalmist. Jonah also called to the Lord from the depths of the sea, in the belly of a fish, *"I called to you from the land of the dead and, Lord, you heard me"* (Jonah 2:2 NLT). There is no place too deep, too dark, or too far for Him to hear our voice calling.

A dear friend penned these words…

> Come, my little one, have no fear.
>
> Pray to me because I hear.
>
> Trust in God to lead the way,
>
> Go to Him in prayer each day.
>
> So come my little one, just as you are,
>
> Pray to Me because I care
>
> Pray to Me because I hear.
>
> —CAROLYN HARDAWAY

Manley Beasley was a dear friend and faithful man of God. God put Paul and Manley together when Paul was very young in the ministry. They traveled together before Paul got established in evangelism. He is one of the men God used to mentor both Paul and me when we were young and knew little of God or His Word. He was a man of faith. He taught many times on Hebrews 11:1: *"Now faith is the substance of things hoped for, the evidence of things not seen."* He once said, "Great believers are also great doubters." When we're walking with God and listening to His Holy Spirit, we have no problem believing God for anything. However, when we lose our focus and are walking according to our own ways, we are great doubters.

Manley had three terminal diseases when he was a young man: lupus, polymyositis, and scleroderma. He knew he had to get a promise from God or die. He was lying in the hospital bed given no hope of living when God gave him Psalm 128:6: *"Yea, thou shalt see thy children's children."* When no one else believed he would live, Manley believed this promise. His children were very young when God gave him this promise, and he did live to see his children's children. This is the man God used to lead me to the Lord.

The beginning of Psalm 130, says, *"Out of the depths."* It seems like we have to get so desperate before God before we cry out in anguish and really plead our cause before God. We may run to friends and cry to them, yet most of the time all they can do is listen. Friends can't change our dilemma. It goes on to say, *"I cry to you, O Lord!"* Manley knew who to cry to and believe as he lay in that hospital bed with a death sentence. His wife had given up! His doctor had given up! His children had resigned themselves to living without a dad. However, Manley didn't give up! Out of the depths of his soul he cried to the Lord.

> It little matters where we are if we can pray; but prayer is never more real and acceptable than when it rises out of the worst places. Deep places beget deep devotion. Depths of earnestness are stirred by depths of tribulation. Diamonds sparkle most amid the darkness. The more distressed we are, the

more excellent is the faith which trusts bravely in the Lord, and therefore appeals to him, and to him alone.[1]

And the Lord heard Manley's appeals "to Him, and to Him alone" and granted him more years. God's ears were attentive to Manley's cries for healing. He hoped in God's Word and knew God would hear his cry.

Promises to Memorize

For the eyes of the Lord are on the righteous, and His ears are open to their prayers (1 Peter 3:12 NKJV).

This is the confidence we have in approaching God: that if we ask anything according to his will, he hears us (1 John 5:14 NIV).

Then you will call on me and come and pray to me, and I will listen to you. You will seek me and find me when you seek me with all your heart (Jeremiah 29:12-13 NIV).

I sought the Lord, and he answered me and delivered me from all my fears (Psalm 34:4 ESV).

Prayer

Father, my heart is so overwhelmed by Your goodness and mercy. Thank You for answering my cries; for hearing me when I come to You with praise and thanksgiving. Lord, I'm crying for help. I know You are listening, ready to rescue me (Psalm 34:17). Amen.

What promise has God given to you today?

SHELLY KUMMER

Therefore I tell you whatever you ask for in prayer, believe that you have received it and it will be yours (Mark 11:24 NIV).

As a little girl, I have always known that God would bless me with the desires of my heart. It has always been about faith and not allowing the challenges of life to stop me from believing. To be married to an amazing man, I am! Having wonderful children, I do! Being blessed with grandbabies, it's the best. A beautiful ranch that makes me so thankful and grateful that when I wake up every morning, I cry. God's promises are put in our hearts, we just need to believe them!

LESLIE RICE

But Jesus beheld them, and said unto them, With men this is impossible; but with God all things are possible (Matthew 19:26 KJV).

This is what I live by—I have total faith and trust in God. He is always with me. That has always given me peace through all situations.

DARCI EWING

For God hath not given us the spirit of fear; but of power, and of love, and of a sound mind (2 Timothy 1:7 KJV).

This has been a vital promise from God that has radically impacted my life. We do not have a spirit of fear. As a matter of fact, God is love (1 John 4:16) and we are created in His image (Genesis 1:27); therefore we have a spirit of love, power and a sound mind and that truth is so empowering. This promise has served me daily as I remember who I am and my responsibility to operate in that truth based on what I say I believe. Even through the most difficult health challenge when everyone around me was full of fear, I was able to operate in the power, love, and sound mind that I have been given. However, this promise is not just for big situations. It's something to be lived daily. If we live in fear, which is so easy to do with all that is going on in the world, we give our power away. I am so grateful that God has given me a spirit of power, love and a sound mind.

ENDNOTE

1. Charles Spurgeon, *Treasury of David, Psalm 130.* https://archive.spurgeon.org/treasury/ps130.php; accessed November 8, 2021.

Chapter 14

GOD, OUR VERY PRESENT REFUGE

God is our refuge and strength, a very present help in trouble.

—PSALM 46:1 NKJV

A refuge is a place of shelter or protection. It's a place of safety. This whole chapter (Psalm 46) reminds us that God is our refuge. He reminds us that He is the One who is in control. No matter what happens on this ball we live on, He will take care of His own. This doesn't mean that we will never face trouble or go through trials. He tells us that in this world we will have tribulations (John 16:33), but we can be of good cheer because He has overcome the world for us.

The second part of this verse is as important as the first: A very present help in trouble. He is available, reachable when we need Him. In this day of automated messages, God is real, personable, and on call. You don't have to leave a message and wait until next Thursday for Him to get back to you. He is very present. He is God with us, remember? He is our very accessible refuge at this very moment. We can turn to Him now.

"As for God, his way is perfect: the word of the Lord is tried: he is a buckler to all those that trust in him" (Psalm 18:30 NKJV). I can take you back to 1987 when God made this promise very real to me. I had just received some devastating news. My heart was broken, and I felt so alone. I was flying from Colorado to Louisiana. I opened my Bible to the book of Psalms. God began to deal graciously with my heart as I read this promise: *"God is a buckler!"* This word "buckler" means shield or defense. I believe He was shielding my heart against anger, unforgiveness, bitterness, and revenge. His word was being tried in my life. This word "tried" means refined. It's like a goldsmith who is putting gold into the fire to purify it. God was allowing this situation in my life to refine me, purify me. God alone knows what's in our hearts. Jeremiah 18 tells us our hearts are desperately wicked, who can know it? God allows situations into our lives to try us to let us know what is in our hearts so we can repent.

As I looked in the mirror of His Word, He began to show me areas of my life where I needed change; I needed to repent. But, Lord, I'm the one who has been hurt! I'm the one who was sinned against! But we must believe that His way is perfect: truth, complete, without spot, undefiled. He can be trusted! I had to acknowledge that I needed to change. I needed His work of grace in my life. I needed to turn my eyes away from anyone who had hurt me and look to my own sin. It wasn't easy. I wanted to blame! I wanted to fume and fuss! I wanted to sit in my self-pity and wallow in it and feel sorry for myself. However, I refused to live like this. I wanted God to expose everything that wasn't pleasing in His sight. I wanted God to take my life and let it be consecrated to Him. I wanted to be a vessel fit for the Master's use. This is my heart today!

Can we pray like the psalmist:

> *Search me, me, God, and and know my heart, test me and know my anxious thoughts. See if there is any offensive way in me, and lead me in the way everlasting* (Psalm 139: 23-24 NIV).

PROMISES TO MEMORIZE

In God is my salvation and my glory; the rock of my strength, and my refuge, is in God. Trust in Him at all times, you people; pour out your heart before Him; God is a refuge for us. Selah (Psalm 62:7-8 NKJV).

The Lord is their strength, and He is the saving refuge of His anointed (Psalm: 28:8 NKJV).

The Lord is my rock, my fortress, and the One who rescues me; my God, my rock and strength in whom I trust and take refuge; my shield, and the horn of my salvation, my high tower—my stronghold (Psalm 18:2 AMP).

But I will sing of Your power; yes, I will sing aloud of Your mercy in the morning; for You have been my defense and refuge in the day of my trouble. To You, O my Strength, I will sing praises; for God is my defense, my God of mercy (Psalm 59:16-17 NKJV).

Prayer

Truly, Lord, You are my refuge and strength, a very present help in time of trouble. Thank You that I have a place to run to when it seems my life is overwhelming. Truly, the joy of the Lord is my strength. You're my place of quiet retreat. I wait for Your Word to renew me (Psalm 119:114). Amen.

What promise has God given to you today?

JENNIFER ROSARIO

But those who hope in the Lord will renew their strength, they will soar on wings like eagles; they will run and not grow weary, they will walk and not be faint (Isaiah 40:31 NIV).

This family vision and journey to Diamond has been much longer than we anticipated. Often, we felt like giving up. Sometimes we felt inadequate. Other times we felt unworthy. But our biggest source of encouragement was knowing that God would not have put us on this path if He didn't have great plans for us in this direction. I wholeheartedly believed that He already had our Diamond-ship laid out, and all we had to do was to keep moving forward. We held on to the promise that he would help us through it all. And now, I believe he has our Double

Diamond-ship laid out. Our vision had expanded into a greater impact than we would have ever imagined. We just continue to hold on to Him and move forward in obedience to His Word.

BOBBIE PURYEAR

And we know that in all things God works for the good of those who love him, who have been called according to his purpose.

Romans 8:28 is a hope-filled, redemptive promise God has given to me, not just for dark seasons of my life, but for every day of my life. I love that this promise starts with, *"And we know."* I may not always feel it, but I know (understand, accept and make decisions based on the fact) that it is true. I love that God shows His sovereignty and strength next, *"that in all things God works for the good."* In every circumstance, even the ugliest, most destitute moments, God is at work. He is doing the work; I am simply the blessed recipient of His good work. And finally, I love that God clearly defines who this promise is meant for, *"for those who love him, who have been called according to his purpose."* This promise is for me, and the multitude of others who love Him and have been called according to His purpose. When I have been helpless, hopeless, defeated, despised, betrayed, beaten down, confused, cheated on, lied to or lied about, God has kept this promise. He has never allowed anything to touch my life that He won't use for my good and His glory. The details of those hard times fade in comparison to the grace and mercy of God's love, His protection, and His peace.

Chapter 15

BE ENCOURAGED: HIS WORDS ARE TRUTH

Every word of God proves true; he is a shield to those who take refuge in him.

—PROVERBS 30:5 ESV

During one of the hardest times in my life this promise gave me such hope and encouragement. Did it take away the hurt? No, but it helped me see how faithful our Father is during times of doubt, unbelief, sadness, devastation, and discouragement. It doesn't say *some* word of God proves true but *"EVERY word of God proves true."* We can stand firm on this truth. He is our refuge! He is our shield! He is a buckler (armor, safeguard, shelter, guard) to those who trust in Him. His love is unconditional.

143

Sometimes family speaks words of encouragement to us. Sometimes friends encourage us, and sometimes we must remind ourselves of God's promises to be encouraged. I tell ladies, "Stop listening to yourself and start speaking (God's truth) to yourself." What do we say to ourselves? Ephesians chapter 5 tells us to address or speak to ourselves in psalms and hymns and spiritual songs, giving thanks to God. We should make melody in our hearts to the Lord. Again, in Colossians, the apostle Paul says to let God's word dwell in us, teaching and admonishing each other and ourselves, singing psalms and hymns and spiritual songs with thanksgiving in our hearts to God. Our words should always be words of encouragement—building each other up, not tearing each other down. When we are thankful, our words will be words that are encouraging, and they will be words that speak blessing. Remember, every word of God proves true. We need to encourage one another with God's truth.

I have been encouraged by so many people. One particular instance that stands out is when an evangelist called me during a time of discouragement and heartache. I didn't know him very well, at the time, yet he took time to call me. Paul was in Russia on a mission trip, so I was by myself. This evangelist said, "Don't say anything. I just want to tell you that it's going to be okay. You are a child of God. He has you on His heart. He is going to make something good out of this. Be encouraged." He didn't call me to feel sorry for me or let me know how bad things were. He called to encourage me.

Friend, you will never know this side of Heaven what your encouraging words mean to a person. If God puts someone on your heart, stop what you are doing and give them a call, sing them a song, pray for them, laugh or cry with them. Let them know there is someone thinking about them. This may be the very hope they need. A dear friend, who was dying with cancer, called me one day and said, "Sing to me." She didn't say, "Talk to me." She just wanted me to sing to her. As I sang, she was encouraged. I not only encouraged her, but I was greatly encouraged. This is what God's Word says we should do: speak to ourselves and to each other in songs that encourage and edify, songs that glorify the Lord and lift those who have need. And speak His word to one another because *"every word of God proves true."*

PROMISES TO MEMORIZE

Have I not commanded you? Be strong and courageous. Do not be frightened, and do not be dismayed, for the Lord your God is with you wherever you go (Joshua 1:9 ESV).

For God gave us a spirit not of fear but of power and love and self-control (2 Timothy 1:7 ESV).

Trust in the LORD and do good; dwell in the land and befriend faithfulness. Delight yourself in the Lord, and he will give you the desires of your heart. Commit your way to the LORD; trust in him, and he will act (Psalm 37:3-5 ESV).

I will lift up my eyes to the hills--from whence comes my help? My help comes from the Lord, who made heaven and earth. He will not allow your foot to be moved; He who keeps you will not slumber. Behond,

He who keeps Israel shall neither slumber nor sleep.
The Lord is your keeper; the Lord is your shade at
your right hand. The sun shall not strike you by day,
nor the moon by night. The Lord shall preserve you
from all evil; He shall preserve your soul. The Lord
shall preserve your going out and your comng in
from this time forth, and even forevermore (Psalm
121:1-8 NKJV).

Therefore I tell you, whatever you ask in prayer,
believe that you have received it, and it will be yours
(Mark 11:24 NIV).

The Lord is my strength and my shield; in him
my heart trusts, and I am helped; my heart exults,
and with my song I give thanks to him (Psalm 28:7
ESV).

Prayer

Father, as David said in his Psalm, You are my
strength. You are the One who shields me, my
helper always. I will continually give You thanks.
You, Lord, are the One my heart will trust in.
When I doubt, Lord, remind me of Your promises.
Thank You (Psalm 28:7). Amen.

What promise has God given to you today?

RACHEL HERSHELMAN

Trust in the Lord with all your heart, and do not
lean on your own understanding. In all your ways

acknowledge him, and he will make straight your paths (Proverbs 3:5-6 ESV).

As I've held onto this scripture throughout the years, I believe that I keep learning more and more about what it looks like to trust God. If God has a love language, I think it would be trust. Learning to trust means exactly that: it's a choice to believe that God knows what's best for me and to surrender to His plans not my own. His promise is that He will guide my every step and lead me in every decision that I make. Choosing to trust Him displays that I believe His word with my whole heart. I know that in my flesh I am so limited and blind and have had too many days where I relied on myself instead of Him. I've experienced how He leads me daily and how much power is in Him! So, when my flesh attempts to lead me, I mediate on this scripture and am reminded of His promise to me!

ROBIN CARROLL

Therefore I say unto you, What things soever ye desire, when ye pray, believe that ye receive them, and ye shall have them (Mark 11:24 KJV).

This promise was given to me after my healing. I was scheduled for surgery for a long-term injury. Right before my surgery, I woke up one morning completely healed. God had reached down His healing hand and touched my back. I needed a promise I could hold onto during times of doubt, and this is the promise God gave me. I didn't want the nay-sayers to discourage me from believing and knowing God is the One who healed me...thus, the promise of God. I know He healed me, and I will stand on this promise, no matter what. When doubt tries to enter my mind, I will sing God's praises and remind Him of His promise to me. And He left an indent (mark) on my L3-4 vertebrae which looks and feels like a thumbprint! I choose to believe it's God's thumbprint to remind me, daily, of His healing power.

JOEY YADAO

Isaiah 61...the whole chapter.

Going platinum was one of the most challenging times of my life. We were so broke and my life was broken—having a baby out of wedlock, Shane not being able to bring in more than $11 an hour. We were living on our own in Hawaii...that's where all the black scars on my knees come from.

But I found Isaiah 61! It was at my second FED. Ron Puryear did his whole talk on Isaiah 61. He said he felt that this is what the Lord was doing and was going to do, and I took that and ran with it. That was and is the promise that got deposited in my spirit. It was more than just a promise; it gave me the strength to accomplish my mission. Every day I read it in the morning before work to remind me who I am (His anointed) and my mission for Him (what I was called to do on a daily basis). It is a promise that if I'd obey, He will be glorified!

All the promises that are mentioned in this chapter, that came with co-laboring with Him, were just a "hope" at that time. Standing on HIS Word and, more importantly, activating what He said to do, I've been able to watch everything He talks about here, even with our offspring, come to pass: the promises

He made, double honor, everlasting joy, the prosperity that the Lord has blessed us with. I've seen all those and then some come to pass throughout these years!

Chapter 16

I WILL TRUST, EVEN IF...

Blessed is the man who walks not in the counsel of the ungodly, nor stands in the path of sinners, nor sits in the seat of the scornful; but his delight is in the law of the Lord, and in His law he meditates day and night. He shall be like a tree planted by the rivers of water, that brings forth its fruit in its season, whose leaf also shall not wither; and whatever he does shall prosper.

—PSALM 1:1-3 KJV

Scripture says that when we delight in God's Word, His laws, we shall be like a tree that grows by streams of fresh cool water. The metaphor infers that God's Word refreshes and satisfies like cool clean water. At the right time we *will* bear the fruit of our endeavors.

What a tremendous promise! I don't know about you, but I want the blessing of my heavenly Father. I want to walk in His counsel. I want to delight in His Word. I want to meditate on His Word day and night. I want it to be so much a part of me that I can never get away from it.

> We, as Christians, believe that the Scriptures are God's Word. In this passage of scripture, God promises a life of blessing when we are obedient to His laws. We should delight in His laws. We should mediate on His laws. He separates the righteous from the wicked in this passage. What is wicked? "The state of being wicked; a mental disregard for justice, righteousness, truth, honor, virtue; evil in thought and life; depravity; sinfulness; criminality (Author Unknown).

As I said in the beginning of this book, there are thousands of promises from our heavenly Father. I know there's a promise for your life today. He has a supply for every need you have. Our problem is, we don't ask. Perhaps we lack the faith to believe that He will answer us.

I have this battle of unbelief. If God doesn't answer my prayer the way I want Him to, I hesitate to pray and ask for anything because He didn't answer the way I wanted Him to the last time I prayed. I want my way and not His, at times. I must ask forgiveness for this so often.

When our son-in-law, Mark, was fighting for his life, we as a family continually prayed for his healing. However, God had other plans. He called Mark home. I thought to myself, *Why pray?* Yet, I know we have a loving Father who knows better than we do. Psalm 139 says our days are numbered by God. He formed us. We are fearfully and wonderfully made. God's thoughts toward us are peace and not evil to give us an expected end. Our future is in His hands. Promise after promise is ours to claim. So, I will cling to the promises that my heavenly Father puts deep in my heart. I will trust Him. At the end of the day, prayer is more for us. God knows that we need a way to express our hearts and know someone who cares is listening. The results of our prayers are always left up to His prerogatives.

There's a song by Mercy Me titled, "Even If." As the song says, it's easy to sing when everything is going great, but what about when things go wrong? What if God doesn't save me from the hurt? What if He doesn't save me from the pain? What if God doesn't heal my loved one? We know God is able and He can, but *even if* He doesn't, my hope is Him alone.

Shadrach, Meshack, and Abednego had an "Even If" when they refused to bow down and worship the golden image that Nebuchadnezzar set up. They said to Neb, "*God is able to deliver us out of the fiery furnace, but 'even if' He doesn't, we will not worship or serve your gods.*" As we read in Daniel 3, God not only delivered them, but He was also the fourth man walking in the furnace. Hallelujah! God is able!

We need to say to the Lord, "Lord, You've been faithful. You've been so good to me. Even if You don't answer my prayer the way I want You to answer, I will trust You when my heart is overwhelmed. You said in Your Word that You remember that we are dust, so you know how weak I am. Help me!" Listen my friend, cry to the Lord. He hears. He cares. He loves you.

PROMISES TO MEMORIZE

Trust in the LORD, and do good; so shalt thou dwell in the land, and verily thou shalt be fed. Delight thyself also in the LORD; and he shall give thee the desires of thine heart (Psalm 37:3-4 KJV).

He that trusteth in his own heart is a fool: but whoso walketh wisely, he shall be delivered (Proverbs 28:26 KJV).

O my God, I trust in thee: let me not be ashamed, let not mine enemies triumph over me (Psalm 25:2 KJV).

And they that know thy name will put their trust in thee: for thou, LORD, hast not forsaken them that seek thee (Psalm 9:10 KJV).

Jesus Christ the same yesterday, and to day, and for ever (Hebrews 13:8 KJV).

But my God shall supply all your need according to his riches in glory by Christ Jesus. Now unto God and our Father be glory for ever and ever. Amen (Philippians 4:19-20 KJV).

Let not your heart be troubled: ye believe in God, believe also in me (John 14:1 KJV).

Prayer

Lord, You have truly blessed my life. I want to delight in Your Word. I want to meditate on Your promises day and night. I trust You with my whole being. You are the breath in my lungs and the beat of my heart. I need You every hour, most gracious Lord. Amen.

What promise has God given to you today?

PENNY ALCOTT

I can do all things through Christ who gives me strength (Philippians 4:13 NIV).

We have stood on this verse for decades!

KATHY GALLO

In 1977 I was pregnant with our firstborn. God spoke to me so clearly that I knew He was in control and sovereign over all. With all the excitement and expectations of the expansion of our family and a brand-new baby to cherish and hold, I started walking this new road. The Lord spoke to me through Psalm 121: "*I will lift my eyes unto the hills from whence shall come my help? My help comes from the Lord who made heaven and earth. He will not allow your foot to slip, He who keeps you will not slumber nor sleep.*" Not such an exciting verse for a new expecting Mom, but it's what the Lord had given me.

Daily I would meditate on this verse resting in the sovereignty of the Lord. When the birthing pains came, I recited this verse straight into the delivery room. After an easy five-hour normal birth, finally our son had arrived. Oh, how we rejoiced in this perfect tiny son God had blessed us with! Our hearts rejoiced and were overflowing with thanksgiving and praise. And home we went to enjoy this tiny precious bundle of blessings.

It was a full week of feedings, burping, changing and rocking before my world suddenly stopped. Al left as usual early in the morning to go to work. I had just gotten Jason up from his nap to feed and put him back down. When he was settled again, I made a trip to the bathroom and started to hemorrhage. In a panic, I picked up the phone and called Al. By God's grace he was still at the flower shop and just getting ready to head out on deliveries. God just knew I would have foolishly waited for him to return to call me and bleed to death unwilling to call for help and leave my baby. Instead, he made a bee line home where we would start a horrifying week.

I was in the hospital for 8 long days as a result of an artery being cut in an episiotomy. I endured 5 surgeries in 6 days, many transfusions and feeling like the end was surely near. God suddenly spoke and gave me the peace I would make it through this. He is in control of all and I need to trust and lift my eyes to Him. To the front of my mind came this Bible verse again. Where does my help come from? The Lord! He is in control, and I can rest in Him. He's got this!

Chapter 17

HEAVEN: A PLACE PREPARED FOR US

Let not your heart be troubled: ye believe in God, believe also in me. In my Father's house are many mansions: if it were not so, I would have told you. I go to prepare a place for you. And if I go and prepare a place for you, I will come again, and receive you unto myself; that where I am, there ye may be also. And whither I go ye know, and the way ye know.

—JOHN 14:1-4 KJV

Jesus comforted His disciples with the promise that He would go and provide a place for them. The most beautiful part was this assurance: He would return for them and receive them unto Himself. This promise is for us, His children.

Some religions believe heaven is a place where God lives and where good people go when they die. Yes, Heaven is the place where God is (Psalm 33), but it's not good people who are going, it's redeemed people; people who have trusted Christ as their Lord and Savior. Jesus made it plain when He said He is the way, the only way, the truth, the only truth, and He is the life. No man, woman, boy, or girl will go to Heaven because of their good works or good life, or at least what some consider a good life. There is only one way: Christ.

> *For we know that if our earthly house of this taber-*
> *nacle were dissolved, we have a building of God, a*
> *house not made with hands, eternal in the heavens*
> (2 Corinthians 5:1 KJV).

There is a misconception about Heaven. We don't become angels when we die and go to Heaven. We won't sit around on clouds all day playing harps. Christmas plays always depict angels as little girls with flowing white robes. They are seen more like fairy godmothers than the angels described in the Bible. Angels are not human. They are supernatural spiritual beings who are God's servants.

> Angels are ministering spirits sent to help the heirs
> of salvation. But just as they fulfill God's will in
> salvation for believers in Jesus Christ, so they are
> also "avengers" who use their great power to fulfill
> God's will in judgment.[1]

When I read this, I don't think a fat, little angel could be an avenger with great power. I read about a mighty warrior doing

God's bidding. Michael and Gabriel certainly were powerful angels doing God's will.

What will we do in Heaven? We will sing, work, praise, fellowship, learn, have a new life free from sin, be with Jesus and be reunited with our loved ones. This is something to look forward to in Heaven. Yet, we cling to this life because God has put it in humans to love life.

In the last book of the Bible, Revelation, John was allowed to see a glimpse of Heaven.

> *And I saw a new heaven and a new earth: for the first heaven and the first earth were passed away; and there was no more sea. And I John saw the holy city, new Jerusalem, coming down from God out of heaven, prepared as a bride adorned for her husband. And I heard a great voice out of heaven saying, Behold, the tabernacle of God is with men, and he will dwell with them, and they shall be his people, and God himself shall be with them, and be their God. And God shall wipe away all tears from their eyes; and there shall be no more death, neither sorrow, nor crying, neither shall there be any more pain: for the former things are passed away. ...And he said unto me, It is done. I am Alpha and Omega, the beginning and the end. I will give unto him that is athirst of the fountain of the water of life freely. He that overcometh shall inherit all things; and I will be his God, and he shall be my son* (Revelation 21:1-7 KJV).

God showed John a great city descending out of Heaven, which had the glory of God. He described light that was like a stone most precious. It had a great and high wall with twelve gates, and at the gates were angels. John goes on to describe in detail the gates. He said there was no temple because the Lord God Almighty and the Lamb (Jesus) are the temple. There's no need for the sun or moon because the glory of God will be our light. There will be nothing that will defile or no one WHO works abomination or lies in this city. Only those whose names are written in the Lamb's book of life will be there.

My dear friend, read the last two chapters in the book of Revelation to learn more about your heavenly home. As I am reading this description of Heaven, my heart is rejoicing for those who have gone before me. What joy they are experiencing. What joy we have to look forward to!

An old hymn I have sung for years is, *"When we all get to heaven, what a day of rejoicing that will be. When we all see Jesus, we'll sing and shout the victory."*[2] I've heard preachers make fun of this song saying we should be rejoicing here. Well, yes, we should, but when we get to Heaven, we will know what real rejoicing is. We will sing and shout VICTORY and knowing Heaven is a city, but more than a city, a place but more than a place, for the child of God, it is HOME.

The older I get, the more real Heaven becomes. After all, this is where we as Christians will spend eternity. What is 100 years compared to eternity? Yet, we seem to set our affections on things here rather than where we will spend eternity. Heaven is HOME. This world isn't my home, I'm just passing through, and the older I get, the more Heaven is populated by loved ones and friends.

When Paul's dad was dying, Paul's mom told us he listened to my recording about Heaven over and over. The song was "How Beautiful Heaven Must Be." This song says Heaven is home, a home where we are happy and free; it's a haven of rest for the weary. Jesus said in John 14 that He is preparing a place for us, and where He is, we who are born again will one day be. Life on this earth will be no more. I believe, when death is imminent, we aren't thinking about houses and cars and possessions, we are thinking about eternity. Paul's dad was thinking about eternity. I know we will see him again. Where will you spend eternity? Ask yourself the question: *Am I prepared?* My dear friend, we will take our flight one day. This body of clay will be no more. God will set our spirits free. We will see King Jesus and our loved ones who are there to greet us. What a day that will be!

> *And just as it is appointed for man to die once, and after that comes judgment, so Christ, having been offered once to bear the sins of many, will appear a second time, not to deal with sin but to save those who are eagerly waiting for him* (Hebrews 9:27-28 ESV).

PROMISES TO MEMORIZE

Nevertheless we, according to his promise, look for new heavens and a new earth, wherein dwelleth righteousness (2 Peter 3:13 KJV).

But now they desire a better country, that is, an heavenly: wherefore God is not ashamed to be called their God: for he hath prepared for them a city (Hebrews 11:16 KJV).

Rejoice, and be exceeding glad: for great is your reward in heaven... (Matthew 5:12 KJV).

For here have we no continuing city, but we seek one to come (Hebrews 13:14 KJV).

He will swallow up death in victory; and the Lord GOD will wipe away tears from off all faces; and the rebuke of his people shall he take away from off all the earth: for the LORD hath spoken it (Isaiah 25:8 KJV).

Enter ye in at the strait gate: for wide is the gate, and broad is the way, that leadeth to destruction, and many there be which go in thereat: Because strait is the gate, and narrow is the way, which leadeth unto life, and few there be that find it (Matthew 7:13-14 KJV).

If ye then be risen with Christ, seek those things which are above, where Christ sitteth on the right hand of God. Set your affection on things above, not on things on the earth. For ye are dead, and your life is hid with Christ in God. When Christ, who is our life, shall appear, then shall ye also appear with him in glory (Colossians 3:1-4 KJV).

Prayer

Lord, I will see You in all Your splendor and glory when I get to Heaven. Truly, eye has not seen, or ear heard what wonderful things You have for me. I thank You for preparing a place for me, that where You are, I will someday be. My heart is overjoyed to know I will also see my loved ones, again. Amen.

What promise has God given you today?

GAIL STOKES

I will extol thee, O LORD; for thou hast lifted me up, and hast not made my foes to rejoice over me. O LORD my God, I cried unto thee, and thou hast healed me. Thou hast turned for me my mourning into dancing: thou hast put off my sackcloth and girded me with gladness; To the end that my glory may sing praise to thee, and not be silent. O LORD my God, I will give thanks unto thee for ever (Psalm 30:1-2;11-12 KJV).

When Billie asked me for my favorite verse, I immediately teared up and knew it was, *"Joy comes in the morning."* Never having studied Psalm 30, where this promise lies, it was necessary to put it in context. You will find when you read it, that you've been there too, not knowing how long it will take for morning to come and is joy going to feel like it did before.

Here are some of God's promises from Psalm 30:

Verse 1: *You have lifted me up, have not let my foes rejoice over me,*
Verse 2: *You healed me.*
Verse 3: *You brought my soul up from the grave, You have kept me alive.*

Verse 5: *His favor is for life, but joy comes in the morning.*

Verse 7: *Lord, by Your favor You have made my mountain stand strong.*

Verse 11: *You have turned for me, my mourning into dancing. You have put off my sackcloth and clothed me with gladness.*

It's our choice how we go through struggles. We can rise up when we fall and stand tall. My daughter, whose innocent husband's life was taken (or: husband was murdered), by violent means, said to me, "It's our choice how we go through this." God's word says He will lift me up, He will turn my mourning into dancing and that *"Joy will come in the morning."*

There are 12 verses in this wonderful Psalm that Gail is holding on to. David, the psalmist, went from the pit of despair to praising God. This is where we must end up if we are going to have any victory in our lives. He cried unto the Lord! Cry! Dear friend, cry to the One who can change your mourning into dancing. This is really a psalm of thanks. David is thanking God for delivering him from his mourning to filling his life with joy and dancing. Joy will come in the morning! Hallelujah!

There is a song by Matt Maher called "Alive and Breathing." The chorus says: "Joy still comes in the morning, hope still walks with the hurting, if you're still alive and breathing, Praise the Lord. Don't stop dancing and dreaming, there's still Good News worth repeating, so lift your head and keep singing, Praise the Lord."[3]

JULIE KONING

I am with you always... (Matthew 28:20).

This is the ultimate promise. Nothing else matters.

ENDNOTES

1. Billy Graham/answers/What Are Angels Like? https://billygraham.org/answer/what-are-angels-really-like/; accessed November 9, 2021.

2. Hymn, "When We All Get to Heaven", https://hymnary.org/text/sing_the_wondrous_love_of_jesus_sing_his; accessed November 9, 2021.

3. Matt Maher, "Alive & Breathing," 2020.

God's Sovereignty
and the Holy Spirit

I have lived, Sir, a long time, and the longer I live,
the more convincing proofs I see of this truth; that
God governs the affairs of man. And if a sparrow
cannot fall to the ground without his notice, is it
probable that an empire can rise without his aid?
—Benjamin Franklin[1]

There are two truths that have been my foundation from the
time I was saved. First is the sovereignty of God. To be truthful,
I believe it was before I got saved that I knew in my heart that
God IS sovereign. I came to this truth after I received a letter
from a friend who put a scripture at the end of her letter that
brought this to my attention. I can't even remember what the

scripture was, but right then and there I believed this truth: God is sovereign! Sovereignty means that God is the supreme authority, and everything is under His control. It means that God has a right to do all things and does all things right. Charles Spurgeon said, *"When you go through a trial, the sovereignty of God is the pillow upon which you lay your head."*[2]

Now, do I act like I believe this all the time? No, but I do believe it! I am like the man who said he believed Jesus could heal his son (Mark 9:24), and then cried and said, "I believe, but help my unbelief." I've cried this so many times. I am so grateful for God's patience and long-suffering to me.

The second foundation upon which I stand and find peace and joy is the Person, work, and ministry of God the Holy Spirit. As much as we need Jesus to be saved, we need the Holy Spirit to live saved. He, Holy Spirit, is the third Person of the Trinity. Jesus said, *"I tell you the truth: it is to your advantage that I go away, for if I do not go away, the Helper* [Holy Spirit] *will not come to you. But if I go, I will send him to you"* (John 16:7 ESV)

Jesus promised a Helper. The Spirit is the *parakletos*, the One who comes alongside. Jesus said He would *"be with you forever… He dwells with you and will be in you"* (John 14:16-17 NKJV). In other words, His ministry is not only permanent but personal.

What does the Holy Spirit do? He convicts sinners of their need for a Savior. He is the regenerator of our human spirits; He draws us closer to the Lord; He helps us pray; He sanctifies us in the Lord, He guides us into all truth; He teaches us all things. He is the One who anoints us with His divine power and is our Helper and Comforter in this life (John 16).

So, knowing that our God is sovereign and His Holy Spirit lives in us, we can stand on His promises. We can trust Him in every situation of life. We may not like everything that happens, and I'm sure we won't, but if we really believe God is the absolute Ruler of this universe, we can rest in this promise:

And we know [with great confidence] that God [who is deeply concerned about us] causes all things to work together [as a plan] for good for those who love God, to those who are called according to His plan and purpose (Romans 8:28 AMP).

ENDNOTES

1. Ben Franklin quote was taken from a speech given at the Constitutional Congress in 1787: Delivered Thursday, June 28, 1787, Philadelphia, PA. https:// www.americanrhetoric.com/speeches/benfranklin .htm; accessed November 9, 2021.

2. Charles Spurgeon quote; https://quotefancy.com/ quote/785357/Charles-H-Spurgeon-When-you -go-through-a-trial-the-sovereignty-of-God-is-the -pillow-upon; accessed November 9, 2021.

FAMILY PROMISES

PAUL EDWARD TSIKA SR.

And an highway shall be there, and a way, and it shall be called The way of holiness; the unclean shall not pass over it; but it shall be for those: the wayfaring men, though fools, shall not err therein (Isaiah 35:8 KJV).

When I was first beginning in ministry in the early 1970s, I realized, as I still do, that it was going to take a miracle from God for me to have a ministry. Without a Christian upbringing or any formal education in ministry, I knew, and know, I needed God to provide. It was the latter part of this passage that spoke to my heart: *"The wayfaring men, though fools, shall not err therein."* God quickened to my heart that He had put me on that highway of holiness, and He would always make it obvious to me the direction He had for my life and ministry. He has always, without exception, done that for me. Sometimes He's used adverse circumstances, sometimes input from Billie Kaye, and sometimes His still small voice. But everything He's used, He's always made that promise a reality.

GRETCHEN ANN TSIKA RUSH

"For the mountains may depart and the hills be removed, but my steadfast love shall not depart from you, and my covenant of peace shall not be removed," says the Lord, who has compassion on you (Isaiah 54:10 ESV).

A few years ago, Mark and I were traveling in Washington, and I saw a sign that said, *"Though the mountains may crumble my love will not"* Isaiah 54:10. I looked the verse up and loved it. I had no idea in the next couple of years how the verse would come to mean so much to me. When Mark got sick in 2018, my word was "confidence," and this became my verse. I know that God had me in His hands, and I had confidence that He would take care of me no matter what He had planned.

The promise for me in this verse is that everything around me may crumble, go away, fall apart or be taken from me, but the love of my Lord and Savior will not. He will always be there for me, and His peace will be everlasting and surpass all understanding. This has gotten me through a lot of rough days and days and nights where I got through them by knowing that my Lord loves me, has me in His hands, and is never letting go of me!

Meagan Ashley Rush

She is clothed with strength and dignity, and she laughs without fear of the future (Proverbs 31:25 NLT).

This may not be the typical promise, but for me I find the promise to be that the Lord knows my future and has great plans for me. I love being a role model for my niece and nephews. I don't know if my future will consist of me having my own children and family, but whether or not I do, I have my sisters' families. I want to help them understand that the Lord has their futures planned out. I want to lead and be a role model, an aunt who has strength and dignity, and one who laughs, most of the time, at what the Lord has planned for me.

But the Lord said to Samuel, "Do not look on his appearance or on the height of his stature, because I have rejected him. For the Lord sees not as man sees: man looks on the outward appearance, but the Lord looks on the heart" (1 Samuel 16:7 ESV).

This verse means so much to me and always has. I was born with a chromosome deficiency and there are some things that I don't always love about it. But I know the Lord knit me in my mama's womb and He knew what struggles I would have and how I would be shaped. He sees what is on the inside and that truly is all that matters.

MARISSA ALEXANDRA RUSH SEXTON

Take delight in the LORD, and he will give you the desires of your heart (Psalm 37:4 NIV).

Throughout the Bible there are many instances where God has given us promise after promise. Some He talks about being our right hand in life, and others He talks about how He holds our future. However, there is one that stands out to me more than others: *"Take delight in the LORD, and he will give you the desires of your heart."* There have been many moments in my life where this has been proven true, however one moment sticks out the most. I was going through a rather low point in life and not living my life for the Lord. One night I drove back to the house I was staying at for the time being, and I just sat in my car and cried for a while. I remember praying and telling Jesus that I was done with it all. I told him I was ready to meet my husband and I was done playing games. Three weeks later I met the love of my life, my now husband Shane. He came into my life when I was not expecting it.

I had truly given up all hope, but he came in and changed my life. I am grateful to God every single day for Shane and the family he has given me. As thankful as I am, I know I would not have them without Jesus. He is the sole purpose of our family. We have vowed to love, honor, and serve Him in all that we do. He is the ultimate desire of our hearts; without Him we would not be where we are in life. If you would have asked me when I was younger what I wanted to be, I would have told you a wife or a mom, hopefully both. God gave me an amazing marriage and an amazing son, and I could not be more thankful.

SHANE DANIEL SEXTON

But those who hope in the LORD will renew their strength. They will soar on wings like eagles; they will run and not grow weary, they will walk and not be faint (Isaiah 40:31 NIV).

There was a very long period in my life when my faith wavered from past experiences in my life that had me questioning whether there was anyone there for me. This led me to be absent having a relationship with God. When I met my future wife, Marissa, she asked me if I would be willing to go to church with her and mend my faith. I hesitated at first because I did not know if it was worth the time and effort and if it would make any difference. As I renewed my relationship, I noticed that the hardships still came, but they were easier to overcome, and that I never felt like I was alone when going through them. Every day I am so thankful I made the decision to put my trust and faith into God to help me become a stronger person.

MALORY AMELIA RUSH NORTHRUP

The righteous cry out, and the Lord hears them; he delivers them from all their troubles. The Lord is close to the brokenhearted and saves those who are crushed in spirit (Psalm 34: 17-18 NIV).

This verse has been one that I have held onto for many years of my life. Throughout my life I have had struggles that I faced quietly, ones that I only went to God for, and time and time again He proved to me that I am not alone, He is right there.

Whenever I have called upon Him in a time of great distress or worry, He has heard my cry and come to my comfort. During the season of my life that has presented the most struggle both spiritually and emotionally, God has yet again proven to me that His shoulder is there, that He will always be my biggest encourager and my highest form of comfort. As this year has progressed my spirit has felt defeated, but God has humbled me by being the One who I have chosen to run back to.

Whenever I think back to this promise, it allows me to feel the Lord's Spirit, to know that I am not alone; that no matter what it is that is ailing me, the Lord will literally draw near to me to help me through my struggles. I often think back to the particularly troubling times and realize that God has always given me a way to feel comfort—whether that be from Him directly, or from somebody He sends to me. The biggest comfort He has ever sent me to heal my broken heart is my dear husband. God sent Joshua to me after I lost somebody very dear to me and before my dad was diagnosed with cancer. God knew I would need a tangible human to help me through these two massive events in my life, and He sent me just the right person. No matter what you go through, remain confident that God is always right there to be your comfort.

JOSHUA AARON NORTHRUP

Jesus answered, "You do not know now what I am doing, but later you will understand" (John 13:7 NIV).

This verse is one that people tend to pass over but has been one that I have thought about often in life. Wherever I have gone in life God has paved the way. God has provided no matter if I knew what He was doing or not. Anytime I have doubted myself or where I am in life, God has shown me in some way that His will would be done. When the time has come to a point of understanding, I have always been able to look back and see just how God led me there.

PAUL EDWARD AND MELANIE ELAINE TSIKA

It's nearly impossible for us to choose just one promise that we live by. Each of these builds on the other.

> *Trust in the Lord with all your heart, and do not lean on your own understanding. In all your ways acknowledge him, and he will make straight your paths* (Proverbs 3:5-6 ESV).

Promise: We can put our confidence in God, even when we cannot understand or see what's really happening. He will promise to guide us.

> *Do not be anxious about anything, but in everything by prayer and supplication with thanksgiving let your requests be made known to God. And the peace of God, which surpasses all understanding, will guard your hearts and your minds in Christ Jesus. Finally, brothers, whatever is true, whatever is honorable, whatever is just, whatever is pure, whatever is lovely, whatever is commendable, if there is*

any excellence, if there is anything worthy of praise, think about these things (Philippians 4:6-8 ESV).

Promise: We know that God will take care of things that we yield to Him, and He will guard our hearts. We should focus on what is good and praise God for those things. It helps our gratitude level.

I can do all things through Him who strengthens me (Philippians 4:13 NKJV).

Promise: There's nothing we have to do that He doesn't give us the strength to make it through.

My God will supply every need according to His riches in glory in Christ Jesus (Philippians 4:19 NKJV).

Promise: His supply is endless, and He meets our needs.

So now wrap your heart tightly around the hope that lives within us, knowing that God always keeps his promises! (Hebrews 10:23 The Passion Translation).

Promise: We know that if God said it, He will deliver!

CATHERINE EMILY TSIKA MCDONALD

His massive arms are wrapped around you, protecting you. You can run under his covering of majesty and hide. His arms of faithfulness are a shield keeping you from harm (Psalm 91:4 The Passion Translation).

Psalm 91 is an entire passage of a promise in scripture that I hold near to my heart. When I am feeling defeated, scared or just want to feel near to Him, I remember the promises in this scripture. Psalm 91:4 from The Passion Translation says, "*His massive arms are wrapped around you, protecting you. You can run under his covering of majesty and hide. His arms of faithfulness are a shield keeping you from harm.*" I am grateful to have these promises from the Lord of protection from the enemy or even myself. I look back at some of the trials I have faced and remember those times I cried out after reading this scripture. In those times I knew the Father was right there covering me with His wings and embracing me like only He can do. Knowing this promise throughout my life and for the days ahead helps me to feel safe and secure in Him.

JONATHAN MCDONALD

Trust in the LORD with all your heart and lean not on your own understanding; in all your ways submit to him, and he will make your paths straight. (Proverbs 3:5-6 NIV).

This verse is a constant reminder that putting my trust in the Lord leaves no room for doubt, leaning on His understand allows no room for error, and the path I may choose over Christ's could lead to death.

DEMETRI PAUL AND KALEIGH TSIKA

The promise that we have been living by is found in Ecclesiastes 3:1(NIV): *"There is a time for everything, and a season for every activity under the heavens."*

Being in a world where you want it and you want it now, everything is in God's perfect timing. You are where you are, doing what you are doing, and in the situations that you are in is because that is exactly where you need to be. God is not surprised by anything, and He has ordained your every step. Do not take the season you are in for granted. Be thankful for, and embrace, the season that you are in.

WILLIAM TRACE MORRIS

Therefore everyone who hears these words of mine and puts them into practice is like a wise man who built his house on the rock. The rain came down, the streams rose, and the winds blew and beat against that house; yet it did not fall, because it had its foundation on the rock (Matthew 7:24-25 NIV).

This is my favorite promise from God because it deals with a lot of different topics. Any man can build a house, but to do it properly takes quality time and effort. Then once you have it built, it's tested and tried throughout the years on how it was built.

Another reason why I love this promise is because it only takes one person to do the job right, but if it is built properly and taken care of properly, then it will last for many generations to come. So not only am I building a firm foundation for myself, but also for my family, my grandchildren, and several generations down the line. All with the promise that if we stay faithful and true to His word, and build that firm foundation in our hearts, then He will bless all of us in His timing.

MARLEE KAYE TSIKA MORRIS

And I will ask the Father, and he will give you another advocate to help you and be with you forever—the Spirit of truth. The world cannot accept him, because it neither sees him nor knows him. But you know him, for he lives with you and will be in you (John 14:16-17 NIV).

One of the greatest gifts that God has given us is the power of the Holy Spirit. This promise is so powerful because of the characteristics that come with it. The discernment, power of healing and prayer, understanding, and wisdom just to name a few. As the wife and mom of the home, it is my responsibility to set the thermostat of peace in the hearts of my family.

One of my favorite things about having the Holy Spirit living within me is the discernment about situations that are happening around me. Having this discernment alone has provided protection and peace in my heart along with my husband and unborn son. Trusting the Lord in those situations is what creates the life we have been given.

BRYAN EZEKIEL AND PAXTON TSIKA

Give your entire attention to what God is doing right now, and don't get worked up about what may or may not happen tomorrow. God will help you deal with whatever hard things come up when the time comes (Matthew 6:34 The Message).

We have recently made this a family promise that we cling to, as we are approaching a new season as parents. Knowing that our future holds many new challenges and unknowns can bring fear or make us feel worrisome. Instead of worrying, we can trust in God's promise that He is our Provider in all areas of life. We know God will provide answers to our questions, peace in our worry, calm in the midst of chaos, and joy through the difficult times.

THOMAS JAMES AND KELLEY LYNNE TSIKA

God is our refuge and our strength, a very present help in trouble (Psalm 46:1 NKJV).

Since 2017, our life has been filled with many blessings and many struggles. This promise has carried us through some of the darkest times and continues to do so. It is amazing how a simple promise can hold so much power.

SHELBY NICOLE TSIKA MARQUARDT

But the God of all grace, who hath called us unto his eternal glory by Christ Jesus, after that ye have suffered a while, make you perfect, stablish, strengthen, settle you (1 Peter 5:10 KJV).

This is my promise that I have held close since I was in high school.

God will perfect, confirm, strengthen, and establish me. He is doing that for me every day. Through every trial I have been through, I have held this promise close, because even though I hurt and struggle, I know that suffering ends. It ENDS. Struggle allows God to work in me, strengthen me, establish me in ways I could not do on my own. I'm so thankful for it. In my hardest of times, I know the suffering will end. It's not my forever. We only suffer "for a little while." And there is a divine purpose in every second of that suffering. We do not suffer in vain. Praise God!

CODY ALAN MARQUARDT

Trust in the Lord with all your heart and lean not on your own understanding; in all your ways submit to him, and he will make your paths straight (Proverbs 3:5-6 NIV).

This promise resonates with me as my upbringing was a mixture of being constantly reminded of God's presence in my life in Catholic school, but also never truly being taught the Gospel. It's so important to remember that although we should always strive to seek a closer and more fulfilled relationship with Christ, it's all too easy to fall into the trap of thinking we must prove our worth to Him. We can do nothing to deserve the gift of salvation except give thanks and glorify our Father's name. I lean on this promise to help me remember that trusting in the Lord and walking in faith is so much more effective and fulfilling than trying to make our way on our own.

THOMAS JAKOB AND KAITLYN TSIKA

Do not be anxious about anything, but in every situation, by prayer and petition, with thanksgiving, present your requests to God. And the peace of God, which transcends all understanding, will

guard your hearts and your minds in Christ Jesus
(Philippians 4:6-7 NIV).

Kaitlynn and I have been married for 2 years now and have been finding our way through the early stages of a young marriage. You start a marriage with vows, which boils down to a promise! Some days a marriage will test you, tempt you, fight you; but even through the hardship of whatever season our marriage will go through, we both realize these vows we made to each other are way bigger than the both of us. By prayer and petition, Kait and I will fulfill God's promise, no matter the season we are in. Prayer and having God at the center of our marriage has kept us strong and will keep us strong and bring peace in every situation we bring to Him!

KADIE JEWEL TSIKA

For I am convinced that neither death nor life, neither angels nor demons, neither the present nor the future, nor any powers, neither height nor depth, nor anything else in all creation, will be able to separate us from the love of God that is in Christ Jesus our Lord (Romans 8:39 NIV).

I love these two verses and promise because in this God shows us that He will not only take care of us but love us even when we have sinned and doubted. Nothing can take the love that God has for us away. He will always be there even if we run and try to hide. We may not think ourselves worthy of God's love and you are right. We will never be worthy, but that's why

God's love is so continuous and good! He is the God who will fight for us and love us amid sin.

PROMISES, PROMISES AND MORE PROMISES

ATTITUDE

Thy word have I hid in in my heart, that I might not sin against thee (Psalm 119:11 KJV).

And whatsoever ye do, do it heartily, as to the Lord, and not unto men; knowing that of the Lord ye shall receive the reward of the inheritance: for ye serve the Lord Christ (Colossians 3:23-24 KJV).

And whatsoever ye do in word or deed, do all in the name of the Lord Jesus, giving thanks to God and the Father by him (Colossians 3:17 KJV).

A merry heart doeth good like a medicine: but a broken spirit drieth the bones (Proverbs 17:22 KJV).

Do all things without grumbling or disputing, that you may be blameless and innocent, children of God without blemish in the midst of a crooked and twisted generation, among whom you shine as lights in the world (Philippians 2:14-15ESV).

Finally, brothers, whatever is true, whatever is honorable, whatever is just, whatever is pure, whatever is lovely, whatever is commendable, if there is any excellence, if there is anything worthy of praise, think about these things. What you have learned and received and heard and seen in me—practice these things, and the God of peace will be with you (Philippians 4:8-9 ESV).

Humble yourselves before the Lord, and he will exalt you (James 4:10 ESV).

Do nothing from selfish ambition or conceit, but in humility count others more significant than yourselves. Let each of you look not only to his own interests, but also to the interests of others. Have this mind among yourselves, which is yours in Christ Jesus (Philippians 2:3-5 ESV).

ANXIETY

Anxiety in a man's heart weighs him down, but a good word makes him glad (Proverbs 12:25 ESV).

It is in vain that you rise up early and go late to rest, eating the bread of anxious toil; for he gives to his beloved sleep (Psalm 127:2 ESV).

And which of you by being anxious can add a single hour to his span of life? (Luke 12:25 ESV).

I can do all things through him who strengthens me (Philippians 4:13 ESV).

I will instruct you and teach you in the way you should go; I will counsel you with my eye upon you. Be not like a horse or a mule, without understanding, which must be curbed with bit and bridle, or it will not stay near you. Many are the sorrows of the wicked, but steadfast love surrounds the one who trusts in the Lord (Psalm 32:8-10 ESV).

Let not your hearts be troubled. Believe in God; believe also in me. In my Father's house are many rooms. If it were not so, would I have told you that I go to prepare a place for you? And if I go and prepare a place for you, I will come again and will take you to myself, that where I am you may be also. And you know the way to where I am going (John 14:1-4 ESV).

BELIEVE

But overhearing what they said, Jesus said to the ruler of the synagogue, "Do not fear, only believe" (Mark 5:36 ESV).

Jesus said to them, "I am the bread of life; whoever comes to me shall not hunger, and whoever believes in me shall never thirst (John 6:35 ESV).

May the God of hope fill you with all joy and peace in believing, so that by the power of the Holy Spirit you may abound in hope (Romans 15:13 ESV).

For with the heart one believes and is justified, and with the mouth one confesses and is saved (Romans 10:10 ESV).

Therefore I tell you, whatever you ask in prayer, believe that you have received it, and it will be yours (Mark 11:24 ESV).

BLESSED

Blessed are the poor in spirit, for theirs is the kingdom of heaven. Blessed are those who mourn, for they shall be comforted. Blessed are the meek, for they shall inherit the earth. Blessed are those who hunger and thirst for righteousness, for they shall be satisfied. Blessed are the merciful, for they shall receive mercy (Matthew 5:3-7 ESV).

Blessed is the man who trusts in the Lord, whose trust is the Lord (Jeremiah 17:7 ESV).

Blessed is he who comes in the name of the Lord! We bless you from the house of the Lord (Psalm 118:26 ESV).

Blessed are the pure in heart, for they shall see God. Blessed are the peacemakers, for they shall be called sons of God. Blessed are those who are persecuted for righteousness' sake, for theirs is the kingdom of heaven. Blessed are you when others revile you and persecute you and utter all kinds of evil against you falsely on my account. Rejoice and be glad, for your reward is great in heaven, for so they persecuted the prophets who were before you (Matthew 5:8-12 ESV).

Blessed is the man who walks not in the counsel of the wicked, nor stands in the way of sinners, nor sits in the seat of scoffers (Psalm 1:1 ESV).

But he said, "Blessed rather are those who hear the word of God and keep it!" (Luke 11:28 ESV).

CHOSEN

You did not choose me, but I chose you and appointed you that you should go and bear fruit and that your fruit should abide, so that whatever you ask the Father in my name, he may give it to you (John 15:16 ESV).

But you are a chosen race, a royal priesthood, a holy nation, a people for his own possession, that you may proclaim the excellencies of him who called you out of darkness into his marvelous light (1 Peter 2:9 ESV).

And we know that for those who love God all things work together for good, for those who are called according to his purpose. For those whom he foreknew he also predestined to be conformed to the image of his Son, in order that he might be the firstborn among many brothers. And those whom he predestined he also called, and those whom he called he also justified, and those whom he justified he also glorified (Romans 8:28-30 ESV).

Even as he chose us in him before the foundation of the world, that we should be holy and blameless before him. In love he predestined us for adoption as sons through Jesus Christ, according to the purpose of his will (Ephesians 1:4-5 ESV).

For many are called, but few are chosen (Matthew 22:14 ESV).

CONFESS

If we confess our sins, he is faithful and just to forgive us our sins and to cleanse us from all unrighteousness (1 John 1:9 ESV).

Therefore, confess your sins to one another and pray for one another, that you may be healed. The prayer of a righteous person has great power as it is working (James 5:16 ESV).

Whoever conceals his transgressions will not prosper, but he who confesses and forsakes them will obtain mercy (Proverbs 28:13 ESV).

And every tongue confess that Jesus Christ is Lord, to the glory of God the Father (Philippians 2:11 ESV).

Because, if you confess with your mouth that Jesus is Lord and believe in your heart that God raised him from the dead, you will be saved (Romans 10:9 ESV).

Submit yourselves therefore to God. Resist the devil, and he will flee from you (James 4:7 ESV).

For there is one God, and there is one mediator between God and men, the man Christ Jesus (1 Timothy 2:5 ESV).

I appeal to you therefore, brothers, by the mercies of God, to present your bodies as a living sacrifice, holy and acceptable to God, which is your spiritual worship (Romans 12:1 ESV).

COURAGE

Have I not commanded you? Be strong and coura-geous. Do not be frightened, and do not be dismayed, for the Lord your God is with you wherever you go (Joshua 1:9 ESV).

Be strong and courageous. Do not fear or be in dread of them, for it is the Lord your God who goes with you. He will not leave you or forsake you (Deuteronomy 31:6 ESV).

Be watchful, stand firm in the faith, act like men, be strong (1 Corinthians 16:13 ESV).

Wait for the Lord; be strong, and let your heart take courage; wait for the Lord! (Psalm 27:14 ESV).

The wicked flee when no one pursues, but the righ-teous are bold as a lion (Proverbs 28:1 ESV).

Trust in the Lord with all your heart, and do not lean on your own understanding. In all your ways acknowledge him, and he will make straight your paths (Proverbs 3:5-6 ESV).

I have said these things to you, that in me you may have peace. In the world you will have tribulation. But take heart; I have overcome the world (John 16:33 NKJV).

DEATH

He will wipe away every tear from their eyes, and death shall be no more, neither shall there be mourning, nor crying, nor pain anymore, for the former things have passed away (Revelation 21:4 ESV).

For if we live, we live to the Lord, and if we die, we die to the Lord. So then, whether we live or whether we die, we are the Lord's (Romans 14:8 ESV).

And the dust returns to the earth as it was, and the spirit returns to God who gave it (Ecclesiastes 12:7 ESV).

And he said to him, "Truly, I say to you, today you will be with me in paradise" (Luke 23:43 ESV).

For since we believe that Jesus died and rose again, even so, through Jesus, God will bring with him those who have fallen asleep (1 Thessalonians 4:14 ESV).

For the wages of sin is death, but the free gift of God is eternal life in Christ Jesus our Lord (Romans 6:23 ESV).

He will swallow up death forever; and the Lord God will wipe away tears from all faces, and the reproach of his people he will take away from all the earth, for the Lord has spoken (Isaiah 25:8 ESV).

For as in Adam all die, so also in Christ shall all be made alive (1 Corinthians 15:22 ESV).

DEPRESSION

When the righteous cry for help, the Lord hears and delivers them out of all their troubles. The Lord is near to the brokenhearted and saves the crushed in spirit (Psalm 34:17-18 ESV).

Come to me, all who labor and are heavy laden, and I will give you rest (Matthew 11:28 ESV).

Casting all your anxieties on him, because he cares for you (1 Peter 5:7 ESV).

Fear not, for I am with you; be not dismayed, for I am your God; I will strengthen you, I will help you, I will uphold you with my righteous right hand (Isaiah 41:10 ESV).

For his anger is but for a moment, and his favor is for a lifetime. Weeping may tarry for the night, but joy comes with the morning (Psalm 30:5 ESV).

Answer me quickly, O Lord! My spirit fails! Hide not your face from me, lest I be like those who go down to the pit. Let me hear in the morning of your steadfast love, for in you I trust. Make me know the way I should go, for to you I lift up my soul (Psalm 143:7-8 ESV).

ENCOURAGEMENT

Have I not commanded you? Be strong and courageous. Do not be frightened, and do not be dismayed, for the Lord your God is with you wherever you go (Joshua 1:9 ESV).

For God gave us a spirit not of fear but of power and love and self-control (2 Timothy 1:7 ESV).

Delight yourself in the Lord, and he will give you the desires of your heart (Psalm 37:4 ESV).

I lift up my eyes to the hills. From From whence comes my help? My help comes from the LORD, who made heaven and earth. He will not allow your foot be moved; He who keeps you will not slumber. Behold, He who keeps Israel shall neither slumber nor sleep. The Lord is your keeper; the Lord is your shade at your right hand. The sun shall not strike you by day, nor the moon by night. The Lord shall preserve you from all evil; He shall preserve your soul. The Lord shall preserve your going out and your coming in from this time forth, and even forevermore (Psalm 121:1-8 NKJV).

Every word of God proves true; he is a shield to those who take refuge in him (Proverbs 30:5 ESV).

Therefore I tell you, whatever you ask in prayer, believe that you have received it, and it will be yours (Mark 11:24 ESV).

I sought the Lord, and he answered me and delivered me from all my fears (Psalm 34:4 ESV).

The Lord is my strength and my shield; in him my heart trusts, and I am helped; my heart exults, and with my song I give thanks to him (Psalm 28:7 ESV).

ENVY

A tranquil heart gives life to the flesh, but envy makes the bones rot (Proverbs 14:30 ESV).

Let us not become conceited, provoking one another, envying one another (Galatians 5:26 ESV).

So put away all malice and all deceit and hypocrisy and envy and all slander (1 Peter 2:1 ESV).

Be not envious of evil men, nor desire to be with them (Proverbs 24:1 ESV).

Love is patient and kind; love does not envy or boast; it is not arrogant (1 Corinthians 13:4 ESV).

For we ourselves were once foolish, disobedient, led astray, slaves to various passions and pleasures, passing our days in malice and envy, hated by others and hating one another (Titus 3:3 ESV).

For where jealousy and selfish ambition exist, there will be disorder and every vile practice (James 3:16 ESV).

And he said, "What comes out of a person is what defiles him. For from within, out of the heart of man, come evil thoughts, sexual immorality, theft, murder, adultery, coveting, wickedness, deceit, sensuality, envy, slander, pride, foolishness. All these evil things come from within, and they defile a person" (Mark 7:20-23 ESV).

He is puffed up with conceit and understands nothing. He has an unhealthy craving for controversy and for quarrels about words, which produce envy, dissension, slander, evil suspicions (1 Timothy 6:4 ESV).

A fool gives full vent to his spirit, but a wise man quietly holds it back (Proverbs 29:11 ESV).

Fret not yourself because of evildoers, and be not envious of the wicked (Proverbs 24:19 NKJV).

FAITH

So faith comes from hearing, and hearing through the word of Christ (Romans 10:17 ESV).

And without faith it is impossible to please him, for whoever would draw near to God must believe that he exists and that he rewards those who seek him (Hebrews 11:6 ESV).

Now faith is the assurance of things hoped for, the conviction of things not seen (Hebrews 11:1 ESV).

And Jesus answered them, "Have faith in God. Truly, I say to you, whoever says to this mountain, 'Be taken up and thrown into the sea,' and does not doubt in his heart, but believes that what he says will come to pass, it will be done for him. Therefore I tell you, whatever you ask in prayer, believe that you have received it, and it will be yours" (Mark 11:22-24 ESV).

You believe that God is one; you do well. Even the demons believe—and shudder! (James 2:19 ESV)

The fear of man lays a snare, but whoever trusts in the Lord is safe (Proverbs 29:25 ESV).

And I, when I came to you, brothers, did not come proclaiming to you the testimony of God with lofty speech or wisdom. For I decided to know nothing among you except Jesus Christ and him crucified. And I was with you in weakness and in fear and much trembling, and my speech and my message were not in plausible words of wisdom, but in demonstration of the Spirit and of power, so that your faith might not rest in the wisdom of men but in the power of God (1 Corinthians 2:1-5 ESV).

So we are always of good courage. We know that while we are at home in the body we are away from the Lord, for we walk by faith, not by sight (2 Corinthians 5:6-7 ESV).

I have been crucified with Christ. It is no longer I who live, but Christ who lives in me. And the life I now live in the flesh I live by faith in the Son of God, who loved me and gave himself for me (Galatians 2:20 ESV).

For by grace you have been saved through faith. And this is not your own doing; it is the gift of God, not a result of works, so that no one may boast. For we are his workmanship, created in Christ Jesus for good works, which God prepared beforehand, that we should walk in them (Ephesians 2:8-10 ESV).

For nothing will be impossible with God (Luke 1:37 ESV).

Yet we know that a person is not justified by works of the law but through faith in Jesus Christ, so we also have believed in Christ Jesus, in order to be justified by faith in Christ and not by works of the law, because by works of the law no one will be justified (Galatians 2:16 ESV).

FORGIVENESS

Be kind to one another, tenderhearted, forgiving one another, as God in Christ forgave you (Ephesians 4:32 ESV).

Pay attention to yourselves! If your brother sins, rebuke him, and if he repents, forgive him, and if he sins against you seven times in the day, and turns to you seven times, saying, "I repent," you must forgive him (Luke 17:3-4 ESV).

Judge not, and you will not be judged; condemn not, and you will not be condemned; forgive, and you will be forgiven (Luke 6:37 ESV).

And whenever you stand praying, forgive, if you have anything against anyone, so that your Father also who is in heaven may forgive you your trespasses (Mark 11:25 ESV).

A soft answer turns away wrath, but a harsh word stirs up anger (Proverbs 15:1 ESV).

Good sense makes one slow to anger, and it is his glory to overlook an offense (Proverbs 19:11 ESV).

So, chosen by God for this new life of love, dress in the wardrobe God picked out for you: compassion, kindness, humility, quiet strength, discipline. Be even-tempered, content with second-place, quick to forgive an offense. Forgive as quickly and completely as the Master forgave you (Colossians 3:12-13 The Message).

If we confess our sins, he is faithful and just to forgive us our sins and to cleanse us from all unrighteousness (1 John 1:9 ESV).

Hatred stirs up strife, but love covers all offenses (Proverbs 10:12 ESV).

Then Peter came up and said to him, "Lord, how often will my brother sin against me, and I forgive him? As many as seven times?" Jesus said to him, "I do not say to you seven times, but seventy-seven times" (Matthew 18:21-22 ESV).

FEAR

The law of the LORD is perfect, reviving the soul; the testimony of the LORD is sure, making wise the simple; the precepts of the LORD are right, rejoicing the heart; the commandment of the LORD is pure, enlightening the eyes; the fear of the LORD is clean, enduring forever; the rules of the LORD are true, and righteous altogether. More to be desired are they than gold, even much fine gold: sweeter also than honey and the drippings of the honeycomb. Moreover, by them is your servant warned; in keeping them there is great reward (Psalm 19:7-11 ESV).

The fear of the Lord is the beginning of knowledge; fools despise wisdom and instruction (Proverbs 1:7 ESV).

Therefore, my beloved, as you have always obeyed, so now, not only as in my presence but much more in my absence, work out your own salvation with fear and trembling, for it is God who works in you, both to will and to work for his good pleasure (Philippians 2:12-13 ESV).

For God gave us a spirit not of fear but of power and love and self-control (2 Timothy 1:7 ESV).

There is no fear in love, but perfect love casts out fear. For fear has to do with punishment, and whoever fears has not been perfected in love. We love because he first loved us (1 John 4:18-19 ESV).

Fear not, for I am with you; be not dismayed, for I am your God; I will strengthen you, I will help you, I will uphold you with my righteous right hand (Isaiah 41:10 ESV).

A Psalm of David. The Lord is my shepherd; I shall not want. He makes me lie down in green pastures. He leads me beside still waters. He restores my soul. He leads me in paths of righteousness for his name's sake. Even though I walk through the valley of the shadow of death, I will fear no evil, for you are with me; your rod and your staff, they comfort me. You prepare a table before me in the presence of my enemies; you anoint my head with oil; my cup overflows. Surely goodness and mercy shall follow me all the days of my life, and I shall dwell in the house of the LORD forever (Psalm 23:1-6 ESV).

I sought the Lord, and he answered me and delivered me from all my fears (Psalm 34:4 ESV).

GENEROSITY

One gives freely, yet grows all the richer; another withholds what he should give, and only suffers want. Whoever brings blessing will be enriched, and one who waters will himself be watered (Proverbs 11:24-25 ESV).

For where your treasure is, there your heart will be also (Matthew 6:21 ESV).

Whoever is generous to the poor lends to the Lord, and he will repay him for his deed (Proverbs 19:17 ESV).

Whoever closes his ear to the cry of the poor will himself call out and not be answered (Proverbs 21:13 ESV).

Each one must give as he has decided in his heart, not reluctantly or under compulsion, for God loves a cheerful giver (2 Corinthians 9:7 ESV).

For God so loved the world, that he gave his only Son, that whoever believes in him should not perish but have eternal life (John 3:16 ESV).

Do not neglect to do good and to share what you have, for such sacrifices are pleasing to God (Hebrews 13:16 ESV).

GRIEF

Blessed are those who mourn, for they shall be comforted (Matthew 5:4 ESV).

He heals the brokenhearted and binds up their wounds (Psalm 147:3 ESV).

He will wipe away every tear from their eyes, and death shall be no more, neither shall there be mourning, nor crying, nor pain anymore, for the former things have passed away (Revelation 21:4 ESV).

I have said these things to you, that in me you may have peace. In the world you will have tribulation. But take heart; I have overcome the world (John 16:33 ESV).

For everything there is a season, and a time for every matter under heaven: a time to be born, and a time to die; a time to plant, and a time to pluck up what is planted; a time to kill, and a time to heal; a time to break down, and a time to build up; a time to weep, and a time to laugh; a time to mourn, and a time to dance; a time to cast away stones, and a time to gather stones together; a time to embrace, and a time to refrain from embracing; a time to seek, and a time to lose; a time to keep, and a time to cast away; a time to tear, and a time to sew; a time to keep silence, and a time to speak; a time to love, and a time to hate; a time for war, and a time for peace. (Ecclesiastes 3:1-8 ESV).

Come to me, all who labor and are heavy laden, and I will give you rest. Take my yoke upon you, and learn from me, for I am gentle and lowly in heart, and you will find rest for your souls. For my yoke is easy, and my burden is light (Matthew 11:28-30 ESV).

All praise to the God and Father of our Master, Jesus the Messiah! Father of all mercy! God of all healing counsel! He comes alongside us when we go through hard times, and before you know it, he brings us alongside someone else who is going through hard times so that we can be there for that person just as God was there for us. We have plenty of hard times that come from following the Messiah, but no more so than the good times of his healing comfort—we get a full measure of that, too.

When we suffer for Jesus, it works out for your healing and salvation. If we are treated well, given a helping hand and encouraging word, that also works to your benefit, spurring you on, face forward, unflinching. Your hard times are also our hard times. When we see that you're just as willing to endure the hard times as to enjoy the good times, we know you're going to make it, no doubt about it (2 Corinthians 1:3-7 The Message).

GUILT

There is therefore now no condemnation for those who are in Christ Jesus (Romans 8:1 ESV).

Therefore, since we have been justified by faith, we have peace with God through our Lord Jesus Christ (Romans 5:1 ESV).

Submit yourselves therefore to God. Resist the devil, and he will flee from you (James 4:7).

The Lord is not slow to fulfill his promise as some count slowness, but is patient toward you, not wishing that any should perish, but that all should reach repentance (2 Peter 3:9 ESV).

For we do not have a high priest who is unable to sympathize with our weaknesses, but one who in every respect has been tempted as we are, yet without sin (Hebrews 4:15 ESV).

For godly grief produces a repentance that leads to salvation without regret, whereas worldly grief produces death (2 Corinthians 7:10 ESV).

For the wages of sin is death, but the free gift of God is eternal life in Christ Jesus our Lord (Romans 6:23 ESV).

He is the propitiation for our sins, and not for ours only but also for the sins of the whole world (1 John 2:2 ESV).

HEAVEN

He will wipe away every tear from their eyes, and death shall be no more, neither shall there be mourning, nor crying, nor pain anymore, for the former things have passed away (Revelation 21:4 ESV).

But, as it is written, "What no eye has seen, nor ear heard, nor the heart of man imagined, what God has prepared for those who love him" (1 Corinthians 2:9 ESV).

And he said to him, "Truly, I say to you, today you will be with me in paradise" (Luke 23:43 ESV).

Do not lay up for yourselves treasures on earth, where moth and rust destroy and where thieves break in and steal, but lay up for yourselves treasures in heaven, where neither moth nor rust destroys and where thieves do not break in and steal. For where your treasure is, there your heart will be also (Matthew 6:19-21 ESV).

But now they desire a better country, that is, an heavenly: wherefore God is not ashamed to be called their God: for he hath prepared for them a city (Hebrews 11:16 KJV).

I give them eternal life, and they will never perish, and no one will snatch them out of my hand (John 10:28 ESV).

In the beginning, God created the heavens and the earth (Genesis 1:1 ESV).

In my Father's house are many rooms. If it were not so, would I have told you that I go to prepare a place for you? (John 14:2 ESV).

HOPE

"The Lord is my portion," says my soul, "Therefore I hope in Him!" (Lamentations 3:24 NKJV).

Therefore, having been justified by faith, we have peace with God through our Lord Jesus Christ, through whom also we have access by faith into this grace in which we stand, and rejoice in hope of the glory of God (Romans 5:1-2 NKJV).

Now hope does not disappoint, because the love of God has been poured out in our hearts by the Holy Spirit who was given to us (Romans 5:5 NKJV).

To them God willed to make known what are the riches of the glory of this mystery among the Gentiles: which is Christ in you, the hope of glory (Colossians 1:27 NKJV).

Therefore gird up the loins of your mind, be sober, and rest your hope fully upon the grace that is to be brought to you at the revelation of Jesus Christ; as obedient children, not conforming yourselves to the former lusts, as in your ignorance; but as He who called you is holy, you also be holy in all your conduct, because it is written, "Be holy, for I am holy" (1 Peter 1:13-16 NKJV).

Rejoice in hope, be patient in tribulation, be constant in prayer (Romans 12:12 ESV).

May the God of hope fill you with all joy and peace in believing, so that by the power of the Holy Spirit you may abound in hope (Romans 15:13 ESV).

Through him we have also obtained access by faith into this grace in which we stand, and we rejoice in hope of the glory of God. More than that, we rejoice in our sufferings, knowing that suffering produces endurance, and endurance produces character, and character produces hope, and hope does not put us to shame, because God's love has been poured into our hearts through the Holy Spirit who has been given to us (Romans 5:2-5 ESV).

But they who wait for the Lord shall renew their strength; they shall mount up with wings like eagles; they shall run and not be weary; they shall walk and not faint (Isaiah 40:31 ESV).

And now, O Lord, for what do I wait? My hope is in you (Psalm 39:7 ESV).

So now faith, hope, and love abide, these three; but the greatest of these is love (1 Corinthians 13:13 ESV).

For whatever was written in former days was written for our instruction, that through endurance and through the encouragement of the Scriptures we might have hope (Romans 15:4 ESV).

But if we hope for what we do not see, we wait for it with patience (Romans 8:25 ESV).

Blessed be the God and Father of our Lord Jesus Christ! According to his great mercy, he has caused us to be born again to a living hope through the resurrection of Jesus Christ from the dead (1 Peter 1:3 ESV).

IDENTITY

So God created man in his own image, in the image of God he created him; male and female he created them (Genesis 1:27 ESV).

Therefore, if anyone is in Christ, he is a new creation. The old has passed away; behold, the new has come (2 Corinthians 5:17 ESV).

Before I formed you in the womb I knew you, and before you were born I consecrated you; I appointed you a prophet to the nations (Jeremiah 1:5 ESV).

For I know the plans I have for you, declares the Lord, plans for welfare and not for evil, to give you a future and a hope (Jeremiah 29:11 ESV).

But you are a chosen race, a royal priesthood, a holy nation, a people for his own possession, that you may proclaim the excellencies of him who called you out of darkness into his marvelous light (1 Peter 2:9 ESV).

I have been crucified with Christ. It is no longer I who live, but Christ who lives in me. And the life I now live in the flesh I live by faith in the Son of God, who loved me and gave himself for me (Galatians 2:20 ESV).

Now you are the body of Christ and individually members of it (1 Corinthians 12:27 ESV).

See what kind of love the Father has given to us, that we should be called children of God; and so we are. The reason why the world does not know us is that it did not know him. Beloved, we are God's children now, and what we will be has not yet appeared; but we know that when he appears we shall be like him, because we shall see him as he is. And everyone who thus hopes in him purifies himself as he is pure (1 John 3:1-3 ESV).

Or do you not know that your body is a temple of the Holy Spirit within you, whom you have from God? You are not your own, for you were bought with a price. So glorify God in your body (1 Corinthians 6:19-20 ESV).

For we are his workmanship, created in Christ Jesus for good works, which God prepared beforehand, that we should walk in them (Ephesians 2:10 ESV).

If then you have been raised with Christ, seek the things that are above, where Christ is, seated at the right hand of God. Set your minds on things that are above, not on things that are on earth. For you have died, and your life is hidden with Christ in God. When Christ who is your life appears, then you also will appear with him in glory (Colossians 3:1-4 ESV).

No longer do I call you servants, for the servant does not know what his master is doing; but I have called you friends, for all that I have heard from my Father I have made known to you (John 15:15 ESV).

For as many of you as were baptized into Christ have put on Christ. There is neither Jew nor Greek, there is neither slave nor free, there is no male and female, for you are all one in Christ Jesus. And if you are Christ's, then you are Abraham's offspring, heirs according to promise (Galatians 3:27-29 ESV).

To put off your old self, which belongs to your former manner of life and is corrupt through deceitful desires, and to be renewed in the spirit of your minds, and to put on the new self, created after the likeness of God in true righteousness and holiness (Ephesians 4:22-24 ESV).

I am the vine; you are the branches. Whoever abides in me and I in him, he it is that bears much fruit, for apart from me you can do nothing (John 15:5 ESV). *But he who is joined to the Lord becomes one spirit with him* (1 Corinthians 6:17 ESV).

But in your hearts honor Christ the Lord as holy, always being prepared to make a defense to anyone who asks you for a reason for the hope that is in you; yet do it with gentleness and respect (1 Peter 3:15 ESV).

Blessed be the God and Father of our Lord Jesus Christ, who has blessed us in Christ with every spiritual blessing in the heavenly places, even as he chose us in him before the foundation of the world, that we should be holy and blameless before him. In love he predestined us for adoption to himself as sons through Jesus Christ, according to the purpose of his will, to the praise of his glorious grace, with which he has blessed us in the Beloved. In him we have redemption through his blood, the forgiveness of our trespasses, according to the riches of his grace, which he lavished upon us, in all wisdom and insight making known to us the mystery of his will, according to his purpose, which he set forth in Christ as a plan for the fullness of time, to unite all things in him, things in heaven and things on earth. (Ephesians 1:3-10 ESV).

INSECURITY

You are altogether beautiful, my love; there is no flaw in you (Song of Solomon 4:7 ESV).

The thief comes only to steal and kill and destroy. I came that they may have life and have it abundantly (John 10:10 ESV).

And you will know the truth, and the truth will set you free (John 8:32 ESV).

For you formed my inward parts; you knitted me together in my mother's womb. I praise you, for I am fearfully and wonderfully made. Wonderful are your works; my soul knows it very well. My frame was not hidden from you, when I was being made in secret, intricately woven in the depths of the earth. Your eyes saw my unformed substance; in your book were written, every one of them, the days that were formed for me, when as yet there was none of them (Psalm 139:13-6 ESV).

O LORD, you have searched me and known me! You know when I sit down and when I rise up; you discern my thoughts from afar. You search out my path and my lying down and are acquainted with all my ways. Even before a word is on my tongue, behold, O LORD, you know it altogether. You hem me in, behind and before, and lay your hand upon me. Such knowledge is too wonderful for me; it is high; I cannot attain it (Psalm 139:1-16 ESV).

IRRITABLE

Love is patient and kind; love does not envy or boast; it is not arrogant or rude. It does not insist on its own way; it is not irritable or resentful; it does not rejoice at wrongdoing, but rejoices with the truth. Love bears all things, believes all things, hopes all things, endures all things. Love never ends. As for prophecies, they will pass away; as for tongues, they will cease; as for knowledge, it will pass away (1 Corinthians 13:4-8 ESV).

Put on then, as God's chosen ones, holy and beloved, compassionate hearts, kindness, humility, meekness, and patience (Colossians 3:12 ESV).

A soft answer turns away wrath, but a harsh word stirs up anger (Proverbs 15:1 ESV).

For the anger of man does not produce the righteousness of God (James 1:20 ESV).

Whoever keeps his mouth and his tongue keeps himself out of trouble (Proverbs 21:23 ESV).

JEALOUSY

For where jealousy and selfish ambition exist, there will be disorder and every vile practice (James 3:16 ESV).

Wrath is cruel, anger is overwhelming, but who can stand before jealousy? (Proverbs 27:4 ESV).

For the whole law is fulfilled in one word: "You shall love your neighbor as yourself." But if you bite and devour one another, watch out that you are not consumed by one another (Galatians 5:14-15 ESV).

I appeal to you therefore, brothers, by the mercies of God, to present your bodies as a living sacrifice, holy and acceptable to God, which is your spiritual worship. Do not be conformed to this world, but be transformed by the renewal of your mind, that by testing you may discern what is the will of God, what is good and acceptable and perfect (Romans 12:1-2 ESV).

A false witness will not go unpunished, and he who breathes out lies will not escape (Proverbs 19:5 ESV).

Do nothing from rivalry or conceit, but in humility count others more significant than yourselves (Philippians 2:3 ESV).

So flee youthful passions and pursue righteousness, faith, love, and peace, along with those who call on the Lord from a pure heart (2 Timothy 2:22 ESV).

Now the works of the flesh are evident: sexual immorality, impurity, sensuality, idolatry, sorcery, enmity, strife, jealousy, fits of anger, rivalries, dissensions, divisions, envy, drunkenness, orgies, and things like these. I warn you, as I warned you before, that those who do such things will not inherit the kingdom of God. But the fruit of the Spirit is love, joy, peace, patience, kindness, goodness, faithfulness, gentleness, self-control; against such things there is no law. And those who belong to Christ Jesus have crucified the flesh with its passions and desires (Galatians 5:19-24 ESV).

For jealousy makes a man furious, and he will not spare when he takes revenge (Proverbs 6:34 ESV).

But the fruit of the Spirit is love, joy, peace, patience, kindness, goodness, faithfulness, gentleness, self-control; against such things there is no law (Galatians 5:22-23 ESV).

So now faith, hope, and love abide, these three; but the greatest of these is love (1 Corinthians 13:13 ESV).

JESUS

For God so loved the world, that he gave his only Son, that whoever believes in him should not perish but have eternal life (John 3:16 ESV).

And the Word became flesh and dwelt among us, and we have seen his glory, glory as of the only Son from the Father, full of grace and truth (John 1:14).

Jesus said to him, "I am the way, and the truth, and the life. No one comes to the Father except through me" (John 14:6) *ESV.*

In the beginning was the Word, and the Word was with God, and the Word was God (John 1:1 ESV).

For to us a child is born, to us a son is given; and the government shall be upon his shoulder, and his name shall be called Wonderful Counselor, Mighty God, Everlasting Father, Prince of Peace (Isaiah 9:6 ESV).

And there is salvation in no one else, for there is no other name under heaven given among men by which we must be saved (Acts 4:12 ESV).

Jesus said to them, "Truly, truly, I say to you, before Abraham was, I am" (John 8:58 ESV).

For there is one God, and there is one mediator between God and men, the man Christ Jesus (1 Timothy 2:5 ESV).

For the wages of sin is death, but the free gift of God is eternal life in Christ Jesus our Lord (Romans 6:23 ESV).

JOY

Love one another with brotherly affection. Outdo one another in showing honor. Do not be slothful in zeal, be fervent in spirit, serve the Lord. Rejoice in hope, be patient in tribulation, be constant in prayer (Romans 12:10-12 ESV).

May the God of hope fill you with all joy and peace in believing, so that by the power of the Holy Spirit you may abound in hope (Romans 15:13 ESV).

Count it all joy, my brothers, when you meet trials of various kinds (James 1:2 ESV).

Rejoice in the Lord always; again I will say, rejoice (Philippians 4:4 ESV).

But the fruit of the Spirit is love, joy, peace, patience, kindness, goodness, faithfulness (Galatians 5:22 ESV).

Until now you have asked nothing in my name. Ask, and you will receive, that your joy may be full (John 16:24 ESV).

A joyful heart is good medicine, but a crushed spirit dries up the bones (Proverbs 17:22 ESV).

Though you have not seen him, you love him. Though you do not now see him, you believe in him and rejoice with joy that is inexpressible and filled with glory (1 Peter 1:8 ESV).

So also you have sorrow now, but I will see you again, and your hearts will rejoice, and no one will take your joy from you (John 16:22 ESV).

Count it all joy, my brothers, when you meet trials of various kinds, for you know that the testing of your faith produces steadfastness. And let steadfastness have its full effect, that you may be perfect and complete, lacking in nothing (James 1:2-4 ESV).

For the kingdom of God is not a matter of eating and drinking but of righteousness and peace and joy in the Holy Spirit (Romans 14:17 ESV).

This is the day that the Lord has made; let us rejoice and be glad in it (Psalm 118:24 ESV).

Therefore my heart is glad, and my whole being rejoices; my flesh also dwells secure. For you will not abandon my soul to Sheol, or let your holy one see corruption. You make known to me the path of life; in your presence there is fullness of joy; at your right hand are pleasures forevermore (Psalm 16:9-11 ESV).

These things I have spoken to you, that my joy may be in you, and that your joy may be full (John 15:11 ESV).

Rejoice always (1 Thessalonians 5:16 ESV).

KINDNESS

Be kind to one another, tenderhearted, forgiving one another, as God in Christ forgave you (Ephesians 4:32 ESV).

The merciful man doeth good to his own soul: but he that is cruel troubleth his own flesh (Proverbs 11:17 KJV).

But love your enemies, and do good, and lend, expecting nothing in return, and your reward will be great, and you will be sons of the Most High, for he is kind to the ungrateful and the evil (Luke 6:35 ESV).

Put on then, as God's chosen ones, holy and beloved, compassionate hearts, kindness, humility, meekness, and patience (Colossians 3:12 ESV).

She opens her mouth with wisdom, and the teaching of kindness is on her tongue (Proverbs 31:26 ESV).

So then, as we have opportunity, let us do good to everyone, and especially to those who are of the household of faith (Galatians 6:10 ESV).

Do not repay evil for evil or reviling for reviling, but on the contrary, bless, for to this you were called, that you may obtain a blessing (1 Peter 3:9 ESV).

Little children, let us not love in word or talk but in deed and in truth (1 John 3:18 ESV).

Whoever pursues righteousness and kindness will find life, righteousness, and honor (Proverbs 21:21 ESV).

LOVE

Let all that you do be done in love (1 Corinthians 16:14 ESV).

Anyone who does not love does not know God, because God is love (1 John 4:8 ESV).

A new commandment I give to you, that you love one another: just as I have loved you, you also are to love one another. By this all people will know that you are my disciples, if you have love for one another (John 13:34-35 ESV).

For God so loved the world, that he gave his only Son, that whoever believes in him should not perish but have eternal life (John 3:16 ESV).

And above all these put on love, which binds everything together in perfect harmony (Colossians 3:14 ESV).

Jesus answered, "The most important is, 'Hear, O Israel: The Lord our God, the Lord is one. And you shall love the Lord your God with all your heart and with all your soul and with all your mind and with all your strength.' The second is this: 'You shall love your neighbor as yourself.' There is no other commandment greater than these" (Mark 12:29-31 ESV).

Greater love has no one than this, that someone lay down his life for his friends (John 15:13 ESV).

Above all, keep loving one another earnestly, since love covers a multitude of sins (1 Peter 4:8 ESV).

So now faith, hope, and love abide, these three; but the greatest of these is love (1 Corinthians 13:13 ESV).

There is no fear in love, but perfect love casts out fear. For fear has to do with punishment, and whoever fears has not been perfected in love. We love because he first loved us (1 John 4:18-19 ESV).

Beloved, let us love one another, for love is from God, and whoever loves has been born of God and knows God (1 John 4:7 ESV).

LONELINESS

Fear not, for I am with you; be not dismayed, for I am your God; I will strengthen you, I will help you, I will uphold you with my righteous right hand (Isaiah 41:10 ESV).

Casting all your anxieties on him, because he cares for you (1 Peter 5:7 ESV).

Be strong and courageous. Do not fear or be in dread of them, for it is the Lord your God who goes with you.

He will not leave you or forsake you (Deuteronomy 31:6 ESV).

Then the Lord God said, "It is not good that the man should be alone; I will make him a helper fit for him." ...And the rib that the LORD God had taken from the man he made into a woman and brought her to the man (Genesis 2:18,22 ESV).

For my father and my mother have forsaken me, but the Lord will take me in (Psalm 27:10 ESV).

Keep your life free from love of money, and be content with what you have, for he has said, "I will never leave you nor forsake you" (Hebrews 13:5 ESV).

I will not leave you as orphans; I will come to you (John 14:18 ESV).

Who shall separate us from the love of Christ? Shall tribulation, or distress, or persecution, or famine, or nakedness, or danger, or sword? As it is written, "For your sake we are being killed all the day long; we are regarded as sheep to be slaughtered No, in all these things we are more than conquerors through him who loved us. For I am sure that neither death nor life, nor angels nor rulers, nor things present nor things to come, nor powers, nor height nor depth, nor anything else in all creation, will be able to separate us from the love of God in Christ Jesus our Lord (Romans 8:35-39 ESV).

Why are you cast down, O my soul, and why are you in turmoil within me? Hope in God; for I shall again praise him, my salvation and my God (Psalm 42:11 ESV).

And I will ask the Father, and he will give you another Helper, to be with you forever (John 14:16 ESV).

MOURN

He will wipe away every tear from their eyes, and death shall be no more, neither shall there be mourning, nor crying, nor pain anymore, for the former things have passed away (Revelation 21:4 ESV).

But we do not want you to be uninformed, brothers, about those who are asleep, that you may not grieve as others do who have no hope. For since we believe that Jesus died and rose again, even so, through Jesus, God will bring with him those who have fallen asleep (1 Thessalonians 4:13-14 ESV).

For the Lord himself will descend from heaven with a cry of command, with the voice of an archangel, and with the sound of the trumpet of God. And the dead in Christ will rise first (1 Thessalonians 4:16 ESV).

I can do all things through him who strengthens me (Philippians 4:13 ESV).

And we know that for those who love God all things work together for good, for those who are called according to his purpose (Romans 8:28 ESV).

Jesus said to her, "I am the resurrection and the life. Whoever believes in me, though he die, yet shall he live" (John 11:25 ESV).

For God did not send his Son into the world to condemn the world, but in order that the world might be saved through him (John 3:17 ESV).

MIND

For those who live according to the flesh set their minds on the things of the flesh, but those who live according to the Spirit set their minds on the things of the Spirit. For to set the mind on the flesh is death, but to set the mind on the Spirit is life and peace (Romans 8:5-6 ESV).

Set your minds on things that are above, not on things that are on earth (Colossians 3:2).

I appeal to you therefore, brothers, by the mercies of God, to present your bodies as a living sacrifice, holy and acceptable to God, which is your spiritual worship. Do not be conformed to this world, but be transformed by the renewal of your mind, that by testing you may discern what is the will of God, what is good and acceptable and perfect (Romans 12:1-2 ESV).

See to it that no one takes you captive by philosophy and empty deceit, according to human tradition, according to the elemental spirits of the world, and not according to Christ. For in him the whole fullness of deity dwells bodily, and you have been filled in him, who is the head of all rule and authority (Colossians 2:8-10 ESV).

For the weapons of our warfare are not of the flesh but have divine power to destroy strongholds. We destroy arguments and every lofty opinion raised against the knowledge of God, and take every thought captive to obey Christ, being ready to punish every disobedience, when your obedience is complete (2 Corinthians 10:4-6 ESV).

You keep him in perfect peace whose mind is stayed on you, because he trusts in you (Isaiah 26:3 ESV).

For God gave us a spirit not of fear but of power and love and self-control (2 Timothy 1:7 ESV).

I will meditate on your precepts and fix my eyes on your ways (Psalm 119:15 ESV).

May my meditation be pleasing to him, for I rejoice in the Lord (Psalm 104:34 ESV).

NEVER GIVE UP

And let us not grow weary of doing good, for in due season we will reap, if we do not give up. So then, as we have opportunity, let us do good to everyone, and especially to those who are of the household of faith (Galatians 6:9-10 ESV).

I can do all things through him who strengthens me (Philippians 4:13 ESV).

For nothing will be impossible with God (Luke 1:37 ESV).

But you, take courage! Do not let your hands be weak, for your work shall be rewarded (2 Chronicles 15:7 ESV).

Fear not, for I am with you; be not dismayed, for I am your God; I will strengthen you, I will help you, I will uphold you with my righteous right hand (Isaiah 41:10 ESV).

For I know the plans I have for you, declares the Lord, plans for welfare and not for evil, to give you a future and a hope (Jeremiah 29:11 ESV).

And we know that for those who love God all things work together for good, for those who are called according to his purpose (Romans 8:28 ESV).

Have I not commanded you? Be strong and courageous. Do not be frightened, and do not be dismayed, for the Lord your God is with you wherever you go (Joshua 1:9 ESV).

But Jesus looked at them and said, "With man this is impossible, but with God all things are possible" (Matthew 19:26 ESV).

NEW CREATION

Do not be conformed to this world, but be transformed by the renewal of your mind, that by testing you may discern what is the will of God, what is good and acceptable and perfect (Romans 12:2 ESV).

For by grace you have been saved through faith. And this is not your own doing; it is the gift of God, not a result of works, so that no one may boast (Ephesians 2:8-9 ESV).

In the beginning, God created the heavens and the earth (Genesis 1:1 ESV).

Therefore, since we have been justified by faith, we have peace with God through our Lord Jesus Christ (Romans 5:1 ESV).

For "everyone who calls on the name of the Lord will be saved" (Romans 10:13 ESV).

For sin will have no dominion over you, since you are not under law but under grace. What then? Are we to sin because we are not under law but under grace? By no means! (Romans 6:14-15 ESV)

ONE GOD

You believe that God is one; you do well. Even the demons believe—and shudder! (James 2:19 ESV).

This is He who came by water and blood—Jesus Christ; not only by water, but by water and blood. And it is the Spirit who bears witness, because the Spirit is truth. For there are three that bear witness in heaven: the Father, the Word, and the Holy Spirit; and these three are one. And there are three that bear witness on earth: the Spirit, the water, and the blood; and these three agree as one (1 John 5:6-8 NKJV).

In the beginning was the Word, and the Word was with God, and the Word was God. He was in the beginning with God. All things were made through him, and without him was not anything made that was made. In him was life, and the life was the light of men. The light shines in the darkness, and the darkness has not overcome it (John 1:1-5 ESV).

"You are my witnesses," declares the Lord, "and my servant whom I have chosen, that you may know and believe me and understand that I am he. Before me

no god was formed, nor shall there be any after me" (Isaiah 43:10 ESV).

"I am the Alpha and the Omega," says the Lord God, "who is and who was and who is to come, the Almighty" (Revelation 1:8 ESV).

I and the Father are one (John 10:30 ESV).

He is the image of the invisible God, the firstborn of all creation. For by him all things were created, in heaven and on earth, visible and invisible, whether thrones or dominions or rulers or authorities—all things were created through him and for him. And he is before all things, and in him all things hold together (Colossians 1:15-17 ESV).

OVEREATING

So, whether you eat or drink, or whatever you do, do all to the glory of God (1 Corinthians 10:31 ESV).

Or do you not know that your body is a temple of the Holy Spirit within you, whom you have from God? You are not your own (1 Corinthians 6:19 ESV).

I have been crucified with Christ. It is no longer I who live, but Christ who lives in me. And the life I now live in the flesh I live by faith in the Son of God, who loved me and gave himself for me (Galatians 2:20).

No temptation has overtaken you that is not common to man. God is faithful, and he will not let you be tempted beyond your ability, but with the temptation he will also provide the way of escape, that you may be able to endure it (1 Corinthians 10:13 ESV).

Submit yourselves therefore to God. Resist the devil, and he will flee from you (James 4:7 ESV).

PARENTING

Train up a child in the way he should go; even when he is old he will not depart from it (Proverbs 22:6).

Whoever spares the rod hates his son, but he who loves him is diligent to discipline him (Proverbs 13:24 ESV).

Fathers, do not provoke your children, lest they become discouraged (Colossians 3:21 ESV).

Behold, children are a heritage from the Lord, the fruit of the womb a reward (Psalm 127:3 ESV).

Honor your father and mother (this is the first commandment with a promise), that it may go well with you and that you may live long in the land (Ephesians 6:2-3 ESV).

Whoever causes one of these little ones who believe in me to sin, it would be better for him if a great mill-stone were hung around his neck and he were thrown into the sea (Mark 9:42 ESV).

And these words that I command you today shall be on your heart. You shall teach them diligently to your children, and shall talk of them when you sit in your house, and when you walk by the way, and when you lie down, and when you rise. You shall bind them as a sign on your hand, and they shall be as frontlets between your eyes. You shall write them on the doorposts of your house and on your gates (Deuteronomy 6:6-9 ESV).

PRAISE

I will praise the Lord according to His righteousness, and will sing praise to the name of the Lord Most High (Psalm 7:17 NKJV).

I will praise You, O Lord, with my whole heart; I will tell of all Your marvelous works. I will be glad and rejoice in You; I will sing praise to Your name, O Most High (Psalm 9:1-2 NKJV).

...I will exalt You, I will praise Your name, For You have done wonderful things; Your counsels of old are faithfulness and truth (Isaiah 25:1 NKJV).

In Him you also trusted, after you heard the word of truth, the gospel of your salvation; in whom also, having believed, you were sealed with the Holy Spirit of promise, who is the guarantee of our inheritance until the redemption of the purchased possession, to the praise of His glory (Ephesians 1:13-14 NKJV).

Therefore by Him let us continually offer the sacrifice of praise to God, that is, the fruit of our lips, giving thanks to His name. But do not forget to do good and to share, for with such sacrifices God is well pleased (Hebrews 13:15-16 NKJV).

Let them praise his name with dancing, making melody to him with tambourine and lyre! For the LORD takes pleasure in his people; he adorns the humble with salvation. Let the godly exult in glory;

let them sing for joy on their beds (Psalm 149:3-5 ESV).

Praise the LORD! Praise God in his sanctuary; praise him in his mighty heavens! Praise him for his mighty deeds; praise him according to his excellent greatness! Praise him with trumpet sound; praise him with lute and harp! Praise him with tambourine and dance; praise him with strings and pipe! Praise him with sounding cymbals; praise him with loud clashing cymbals! Let everything that has breath praise the LORD! Praise the LORD! (Psalm 150 ESV).

Let them praise your great and awesome name! Holy is he! (Psalm 99:3 ESV).

Praise the Lord! Oh give thanks to the Lord, for he is good, for his steadfast love endures forever! (Psalm 106:1 ESV).

Praise the Lord! For it is good to sing praises to our God; for it is pleasant, and a song of praise is fitting (Psalm 147:1 ESV).

With my mouth I will give great thanks to the Lord; I will praise him in the midst of the throng (Psalm 109:30 ESV).

The LORD is my light and my salvation; whom shall I fear? The LORD is the stronghold of my life; of whom shall I be afraid? (Psalm 27:1 ESV).

The law of the LORD is perfect, reviving the soul; the testimony of the LORD is sure, making wise the simple; the precepts of the LORD are right, rejoicing the heart; the commandment of the LORD is pure, enlightening the eyes; the fear of the LORD is clean, enduring forever... (Psalm 19:7-9 ESV).

PROSPERITY

Bring the full tithe into the storehouse, that there may be food in my house. And thereby put me to the test, says the Lord of hosts, if I will not open the windows of heaven for you and pour down for you a blessing until there is no more need (Malachi 3:10).

And you shall remember the Lord your God, for it is He who gives you power to get wealth... (Deuteronomy 8:18).

And God is able to make all grace abound to you, so that having all sufficiency in all things at all times, you may abound in every good (2 Corinthians 9:8 ESV).

Praise the Lord! Blessed is the man who fears the Lord, who greatly delights in his commandments! His offspring will be mighty in the land; the generation of the upright will be blessed. Wealth and riches are in his house, and his righteousness endures forever (Psalm 112:1-3 ESV).

Blessed is the man who walks not in the counsel of the wicked, nor stands in the way of sinners, nor sits in the seat of scoffers; but his delight is in the law of the Lord, and on his law he meditates day and night. He is like a tree planted by streams of water that yields its fruit in its season, and its leaf does not wither. In all that he does, he prospers. The wicked are not so, but are like chaff that the wind drives away. Therefore the wicked will not stand in the judgment, nor sinners in the congregation of the righteous (Psalm 1:1-5 ESV).

QUARRELING

Do not be deceived: Bad company ruins good morals (1 Corinthians 15:33 ESV).

So whoever knows the right thing to do and fails to do it, for him it is sin (James 4:17 ESV).

A hot-tempered man stirs up strife, but he who is slow to anger quiets contention (Proverbs 15:18 ESV).

Remind them of these things, and charge them before God not to quarrel about words, which does no good, but only ruins the hearers. Do your best to present yourself to God as one approved, a worker who has no need to be ashamed, rightly handling the word of truth. But avoid irreverent babble, for it will lead people into more and more ungodliness, and their talk will spread like gangrene... (2 Timothy 2:14-17 ESV).

Pay attention to yourselves! If your brother sins, rebuke him, and if he repents, forgive him (Luke 17:3).

QUIET TIME

But when you pray, go into your room and shut the door and pray to your Father who is in secret.

And your Father who sees in secret will reward you (Matthew 6:6 ESV).

Let not your hearts be troubled. Believe in God; believe also in me (John 14:1 ESV).

To everything there is a season, a time for every purpose under heaven: a time to be born, and a time to die; a time to plant, and a time to pluck what is planted; a time to kill, and a time to heal; a time to break down, and a time to build up; a time to weep, and a time to laugh; a time to mourn, and a time to dance; a time to cast away stones, a time to embrace, and a time to refrain from embracing; a time to gain, and a time to lose; a time to keep, and a time to throw away; a time to tear, and a time to sew; a time to keep silence, and a time to speak; a time to love, and a time to hate; a time of war, and a time of peace (Ecclesiastes 3:1-8 NKJV).

And he said to them, "Come away by yourselves to a desolate place and rest a while." For many were coming and going, and they had no leisure even to eat (Mark 6:31 ESV).

When Daniel knew that the document had been signed, he went to his house where he had windows in his upper chamber open toward Jerusalem. He got down on his knees three times a day and prayed and gave thanks before his God, as he had done previously (Daniel 6:10 ESV).

Pray without ceasing (1 Thessalonians 5:17 ESV).

REDEMPTION

And they sang a new song, saying, "Worthy are you to take the scroll and to open its seals, for you were slain, and by your blood you ransomed people for God from every tribe and language and people and nation" (Revelation 5:9 ESV).

Repent therefore, and turn back, that your sins may be blotted out (Acts 3:19 ESV).

But God shows his love for us in that while we were still sinners, Christ died for us (Romans 5:8 ESV).

For the wages of sin is death, but the free gift of God is eternal life in Christ Jesus our Lord (Romans 6:23 ESV).

For all have sinned and fall short of the glory of God (Romans 3:23 ESV).

I confess my iniquity; I am sorry for my sin (Psalm 38:18 ESV).

My brothers, if anyone among you wanders from the truth and someone brings him back, let him know that whoever brings back a sinner from his wandering will save his soul from death and will cover a multitude of sins (James 5:19-20 ESV).

Bear fruits in keeping with repentance. And do not begin to say to yourselves, "We have Abraham as our father." For I tell you, God is able from these stones to raise up children for Abraham. Even now the axe is laid to the root of the trees. Every tree therefore that does not bear good fruit is cut down and thrown into the fire (Luke 3:8-9 ESV).

SADNESS

Let not your hearts be troubled. Believe in God; believe also in me (John 14:1 ESV).

Is anyone among you suffering? Let him pray. Is anyone cheerful? Let him sing praise (James 5:13 ESV).

Casting all your anxieties on him, because he cares for you (1 Peter 5:7 ESV).

That this is God, our God forever and ever. He will guide us forever (Psalm 48:14 ESV).

A glad heart makes a cheerful face, but by sorrow of heart the spirit is crushed. The heart of him who has understanding seeks knowledge, but the mouths of fools feed on folly (Proverbs 15:13-14 ESV).

SALVATION

He saved us, not because of works done by us in righteousness, but according to his own mercy, by the washing of regeneration and renewal of the Holy Spirit (Titus 3:5 ESV).

For by grace you have been saved through faith, and that not of yourselves; it is the gift of God, not of works, lest anyone should boast. For we are His workmanship, created in Christ Jesus for good works, which God prepared beforehand that we should walk in them (Ephesians 2:8-10 NKJV).

Jesus said to him, "I am the way, and the truth, and the life. No one comes to the Father except through me" (John 14:6 ESV).

But I with the voice of thanksgiving will sacrifice to you; what I have vowed I will pay. Salvation belongs to the Lord! (Jonah 2:9 ESV).

No one can come to me unless the Father who sent me draws him. And I will raise him up on the last day (John 6:44 ESV).

SHAME

If we confess our sins, he is faithful and just to forgive us our sins and to cleanse us from all unrighteousness (1 John 1:9 ESV).

Then the Lord knows how to rescue the godly from trials, and to keep the unrighteous under punishment until the day of judgment (2 Peter 2:9 ESV).

When pride comes, then comes disgrace, but with the humble is wisdom (Proverbs 11:2 ESV).

THANKSGIVING

Give thanks in all circumstances; for this is the will of God in Christ Jesus for you (1 Thessalonians 5:18 ESV).

I will give to the Lord the thanks due to his righteousness, and I will sing praise to the name of the Lord, the Most High (Psalm 7:17 ESV).

Offer to God a sacrifice of thanksgiving, and perform your vows to the Most High (Psalm 50:14 ESV).

Enter his gates with thanksgiving, and his courts with praise! Give thanks to him; bless his name! (Psalm 100:4 ESV).

Oh give thanks to the Lord; call upon his name; make known his deeds among the peoples! (1 Chronicles 16:8 ESV).

Oh come, let us sing to the Lord; let us make a joyful noise to the rock of our salvation! Let us come into his presence with thanksgiving; let us make a joyful noise to him with songs of praise! For the Lord is a great God, and a great King above all gods. In his hand are the depths of the earth; the heights of the mountains are his also. The sea is his, for he made it, and his hands formed the dry land. Oh come, let us worship and bow down; let us kneel before the LORD, our Maker! (Psalm 95:1-6 ESV).

And whatever you do, in word or deed, do everything in the name of the Lord Jesus, giving thanks to God the Father through him (Colossians 3:17 ESV).

Oh, how abundant is your goodness, which you have stored up for those who fear you and worked for those who take refuge in you, in the sight of the children of mankind! (Psalm 31:19 ESV).

He who supplies seed to the sower and bread for food will supply and multiply your seed for sowing and increase the harvest of your righteousness. You will be enriched in every way to be generous in every way, which through us will produce thanksgiving to God (2 Corinthians 9:10-11 ESV).

Therefore, as you received Christ Jesus the Lord, so walk in him, rooted and built up in him and established in the faith, just as you were taught, abounding in thanksgiving (Colossians 2:6-7 ESV).

Continue steadfastly in prayer, being watchful in it with thanksgiving. At the same time, pray also for us, that God may open to us a door for the word, to declare the mystery of Christ, on account of which I am in prison—that I may make it clear, which is how I ought to speak (Colossians 4:2-4 NIV).

We ought always to give thanks to God for you, brothers, as is right, because your faith is growing abundantly, and the love of every one of you for one another is increasing (2 Thessalonians 1:3 ESV).

TRAUMA

I sought the Lord, and he answered me and delivered me from all my fears (Psalm 34:4 ESV).

Come to me, all who labor and are heavy laden, and I will give you rest. Take my yoke upon you, and learn from me, for I am gentle and lowly in heart, and you will find rest for your souls. For my yoke is easy, and my burden is light (Matthew 11:28-30 ESV).

But whoever listens to me will dwell secure and will be at ease, without dread of disaster (Proverbs 1:33 ESV).

For God gave us a spirit not of fear but of power and love and self-control (2 Timothy 1:7 ESV).

I am he who comforts you; who are you that you are afraid of man who dies, of the son of man who is made like grass, and have forgotten the Lord, your Maker, who stretched out the heavens and laid the foundations of the earth, and you fear continually all the day because of the wrath of the oppressor, when he sets himself to destroy? And where is the wrath of the oppressor? He who is bowed down shall speedily be released; he shall not die and go down to the pit, neither shall his bread be lacking. I am the Lord your God, who stirs up the sea so that its waves roar—the Lord of hosts is his name (Isaiah 51:12-15 ESV).

TRUST

And those who know your name put their trust in you, for you, O LORD, have not forsaken those who seek you (Psalm 9:10 ESV).

Some trust in chariots and some in horses, but we trust in the name of the LORD our God (Psalm 20:7 ESV).

Trust in the Lord with all your heart, and do not lean on your own understanding. In all your ways acknowledge him, and he will make straight your paths. Be not wise in your own eyes; fear the Lord and turn away from evil. It will be healing to your flesh and refreshment to your bones (Proverbs 3:5-8 ESV).

Trust in the Lord forever, for the Lord God is an everlasting rock (Isaiah 26:4 ESV).

Our soul waits for the LORD; he is our help and our shield. For our heart is glad in him, because we trust in his holy name. Let your steadfast love, O LORD, be upon us, even as we hope in you (Psalm 33:20-22 ESV).

When I am afraid, I put my trust in you. In God, whose word I praise, in God I trust; I shall not be afraid. What can flesh do to me? (Psalm 56:3-4 NIV).

For I know the plans I have for you, declares the Lord, plans for welfare and not for evil, to give you a future and a hope (Jeremiah 29:1ESV).

There is no fear in love, but perfect love casts out fear. For fear has to do with punishment, and whoever fears has not been perfected in love (1 John 4:18 ESV).

Therefore I tell you, whatever you ask in prayer, believe that you have received it, and it will be yours (Mark 11:24 ESV).

My son, do not forget my teaching, but let your heart keep my commandments, for length of days and years of life and peace they will add to you. Let not steadfast love and faithfulness forsake you; bind them around your neck; write them on the tablet of your heart. So you will find favor and good success in the sight of God and man. Trust in the Lord with all your heart, and do not lean on your own understanding (Proverbs 3:1-5 ESV).

TRUTH

Jesus said to him, "I am the way, and the truth, and the life. No one comes to the Father except through me" (John 14:6 ESV).

So Jesus said to the Jews who had believed him, "If you abide in my word, you are truly my disciples, and you will know the truth, and the truth will set you free" (John 8:31-32 ESV).

The Lord is near to all who call on him, to all who call on him in truth (Psalm 145:18 ESV).

Lying lips are an abomination to the Lord, but those who act faithfully are his delight (Proverbs 12:22 ESV).

Love is patient and kind; love does not envy or boast; it is not arrogant or rude. It does not insist on its own way; it is not irritable or resentful; it does not rejoice at wrongdoing, but rejoices with the truth (1 Corinthians 13:4-6 ESV).

VANITY

Do not be conformed to this world, but be transformed by the renewal of your mind, that by testing you may discern what is the will of God, what is good and acceptable and perfect (Romans 12:2 ESV).

Now the works of the flesh are evident, which are: adultery, fornication, uncleanness, lewdness, idolatry, sorcery, hatred, contentions, jealousies, outbursts of wrath, selfish ambitions, dissensions, heresies, envy, murders, drunkenness, revelries, and the like; of which I tell you beforehand, just as I also told you in time past, that those who practice such things will not inherit the kingdom of God (Galatians 5:19-21 NKJV).

Charm is deceitful and beauty is passing, but a woman who fears the Lord, she shall be praised (Proverbs 31:30 NKJV).

When you discipline a man with rebukes for sin, you consume like a moth what is dear to him; surely all mankind is a mere breath! Selah (Psalm 39:11 ESV).

Let him not trust in emptiness, deceiving himself, for emptiness will be his payment (Job 15:31 ESV).

Turn my eyes away from vanity [all those worldly, meaningless things that distract—let Your priorities be mine], and restore me [with renewed energy] in Your ways (Psalm 119:37 AMP).

For physical training is of some value, but godliness (spiritual training) is of value in everything and in every way, since it holds promise for the present life and for the life to come (1 Timothy 4:8 AMP).

VIRTUE

Finally, brothers, whatever is true, whatever is honorable, whatever is just, whatever is pure, whatever is lovely, whatever is commendable, if there is any excellence, if there is anything worthy of praise, think about these things (Philippians 4:8 ESV).

For this very reason, make every effort to supplement your faith with virtue, and virtue with knowledge, and knowledge with self-control, and self-control with steadfastness, and steadfastness with godliness, and godliness with brotherly affection, and brotherly affection with love. For if these qualities are yours and are increasing, they keep you from being ineffective or unfruitful in the knowledge of our Lord Jesus Christ (2 Peter 1:5-8 ESV).

I therefore, a prisoner for the Lord, urge you to walk in a manner worthy of the calling to which you have been called, with all humility and gentleness, with patience, bearing with one another in love, eager to maintain the unity of the Spirit in the bond of peace. There is one body and one Spirit—just as you were called to the one hope that belongs to your call—one Lord, one faith, one baptism, one God and Father of all, who is over all and through all and in all (Ephesians 4:1-6 ESV).

Whoever walks in integrity walks securely, but he who makes his ways crooked will be found out (Proverbs 10:9 ESV).

Judge not, that you be not judged. For with the judgment you pronounce you will be judged, and with the measure you use it will be measured to you (Matthew 7:1-2 ESV)

WAIT

But they who wait for the Lord shall renew their strength; they shall mount up with wings like eagles; they shall run and not be weary; they shall walk and not faint (Isaiah 40:31 ESV).

For the evildoers shall be cut off, but those who wait for the Lord shall inherit the land (Psalm 37:9 ESV).

Therefore the Lord waits to be gracious to you, and therefore he exalts himself to show mercy to you. For the Lord is a God of justice; blessed are all those who wait for him (Isaiah 30:18 ESV).

Wait for the Lord; be strong, and let your heart take courage; wait for the Lord! (Psalm 27:14 ESV).

WISDOM

Wisdom rests [silently] in the heart of one who has understanding, but what is in the heart of [short-sighted] fools is made known (Proverbs 14:33 AMP).

The [reverent] fear of the LORD [that is, worshiping Him and regarding Him as truly awesome] is the beginning and the preeminent part of wisdom [its starting point and its essence], and the knowledge of the Holy One is understanding and spiritual insight (Proverbs 9:10 AMP).

If any of you lacks wisdom [to guide him through a decision or circumstance], he is to ask of [our benevolent] God, who gives to everyone generously and without rebuke or blame, and it will be given to him (James 1:5 AMP).

For wisdom is better than rubies; and all desirable things cannot compare with her. I, [godly] wisdom, reside with prudence [good judgment, moral courage and astute common sense], and I find knowledge and discretion (Proverbs 8:11-12 AMP).

Happy [blessed, considered fortunate, to be admired] is the man who finds [skillful and godly] wisdom, and the man who gains understanding and insight [learning from God's word and life's experiences], for wisdom's profit is better than the profit of silver, and her gain is better than fine gold. And nothing you can wish for compares with her [in value]. Long life is in her right hand; in her left hand are riches and honor (Proverbs 3:13-16 AMP).

Your commandments make me wiser than my enemies, for Your words are always with me. I have better understanding and deeper insight than all my teachers [because of Your word], for Your testimonies are my meditation (Psalm 119:98-99 AMP).

WORRY

Anxiety in a man's heart weighs him down, but a good word makes him glad (Proverbs 12:25 ESV).

Therefore I tell you, do not be anxious about your life, what you will eat or what you will drink, nor about your body, what you will put on. Is not life more than food, and the body more than clothing? Look at the birds of the air: they neither sow nor reap nor gather into barns, and yet your heavenly Father feeds them. Are you not of more value than they? And which of you by being anxious can add a single hour to his span of life? And why are you anxious about clothing? Consider the lilies of the field, how they grow: they neither toil nor spin, yet I tell you, even Solomon in all his glory was not arrayed like one of these (Matthew 6:25-19 ESV).

And we know that for those who love God all things work together for good, for those who are called according to his purpose. For those whom he foreknew he also predestined to be conformed to the image of his Son, in order that he might be the firstborn among many brothers. And those whom he predestined he also called, and those whom he called he also justified, and those whom he justified he also glorified (Romans 8:28-30 ESV).

ZEAL

It is always good to be made much of for a good purpose, and not only when I am present with you (Galatians 4:18 ESV).

But I discipline my body and keep it under control, lest after preaching to others I myself should be disqualified (1 Corinthians 9:27 ESV).

Brothers, my heart's desire and prayer to God for them is that they may be saved (Romans 10:1 ESV).

And he said, "Come with me, and see my zeal for the Lord. So he had him ride in his chariot" (2 Kings 10:16 ESV).

About the Author

Billie Kaye Tsika grew up in the small south Texas town of Benavides. She had four siblings and a stay-at-home mom. Her dad was an oil field worker. She never realized she was raised poor because of all the Christian love that was in their home.

At the age of 18 she joined the United States Marine Corps in order to qualify for the Peace Corps. But God had other plans. Billie Kaye Rexroad and Paul Tsika met while both serving in the Marine Corps and married April 28, 1966, in Beaufort, South Carolina.

Billie came to Christ following Paul's conversion in the early '70s. They have three children who have been married 31, 30, and 28 years, along with 10 grandchildren and two great-grandsons.

Paul and Billie Kaye have been involved together in ministry since 1971 and have authored several books together, including: *Get Married, Stay Married; Parenting with Purpose.*

Billie Kaye has recorded seven Christian albums along with with her Christmas Classic. She is truly a woman who perfectly fits Proverbs 31:28: *"Her children arise up, and call her blessed; her husband also praises her."*